Man In The Mirror jump-started our Men's Ministry in 2004 by providing a firm foundation through their Leadership Training Center and ongoing education and insight to build our ministry to men. Their training is the best investment our church has made: men are excited about coming to church and so are their women!

W. MARK SHIRLEY, *Men's Ministry Director,*
The MET (Metropolitan Baptist Church), Houston, TX

The vision for men's ministry is not to have a men's group in every congregation! Morley, Delk, and Clemmer have nailed it—the vision is for every man to have a living, growing relationship with Jesus Christ; for every man to be a disciple! This book will give you tools to help make disciples of the men in your congregation and beyond.

DOUG HAUGEN, *Director, Lutheran Men in Mission,*
Evangelical Lutheran Church in America

Two problems plague the church today: biblical illiteracy and lack of male involvement. No Man Left Behind helps solve the second problem by providing a paradigm for churches to develop mature disciples for Christ. Best of all the work is clear, readable, practical, and highly recommended. No Man Left Behind is a men's book for men.

PAUL A. TAMBRINO, EdD, PhD, *Director, Adult and Theological*
Education, First Presbyterian Church of Maitland

In 2003, a friend from my church and I attended the Building a Sustainable Men's Ministry training in Orlando. It was an "AHA" moment for both of us! Pat, David, and Brett share concepts in this book that are "battle-tested." Apply them to your life and ministry with men. Believe me—they work!

KEITH MEYERING, *Director of Planned Giving,*
Bethany Christian Services, Local church men's ministry leader

In the winter of 2003, I was given the opportunity to begin a ministry to the men of FBA. I did not know where to begin. In May 2003, I learned of a training for men's ministry being offered by Man in the Mirror. I attended and invited our new leadership team. It has been "ON" since that weekend. It was definitely the defining moment in our men's ministry.

BRIAN SHULER, *Men's Ministry Pastor,*
First Baptist Church of Atlanta

Our association with Man in the Mirror has transformed our men's ministry . . . It's no longer business as usual. Our motto is: "Every man a leader, every man an influence for Christ, and every man needs a lift!" We may want to add a line: "And no man left behind!"

THE REVEREND DR. H. WILLIAM GREEN, *Associate pastor of First*
United Methodist Church in Cary, N.C.
Recipient of the Ross Freeman Leadership Award in Men's Ministry
(N.C. Annual Conference of the United Methodist Church)

At last! . . . A book that doesn't promise an irresistible men's ministry in five easy steps. It's hard work and someone—you—gets to do it. Revealing what they've learned from helping thousands of churches, Pat, David, and Brett offer an approach that will help you develop a unique—not cookie-cutter—disciple-making ministry for men.

LEARY GATES, *BoldPath Life Strategies*

I had a chance to attend the Leadership Training Center at Man In The Mirror. I love the concept of building an all-inclusive ministry to men. If you want to start a ministry to men, start where they are. No Man Left Behind is a must read.

REX TIGNOR, *People Matter Ministries*

I brought my pastor and several other men to the LTC training classes. We gained tremendous insight into building a sustainable Men's Ministry at East Cooper Baptist Church here in Mt. Pleasant, SC. When we returned, we recruited a group of men and explained the system. We were so excited about what we saw at Pat's Bible study that we copied it. It has been a huge hit with our men. The ECBC "Man 2 Man" Bible study is regularly attended by over 90 men each week. The fruit of this effort has been wonderful. To God be the glory!

RANDY BATES, *Director, Wood Partners*

Men's ministry in our church is no longer defined as those who come to our men's events. Rather, men's ministry is defined by how we are able to disciple a man where he is at. No Man Left Behind is thankfully not another book giving seven steps that will ultimately lead to frustration, aggravation, and despair. Instead, if you will put in the hard work of discipling men—not only will men not be left behind, they will learn to walk with Christ and show others how to walk with Him as well.

MALCOLM H. LIGHT III, *Pastor to Adults,*
Grace Community Evangelical Free Church

No Man Left Behind provides a proven template for building an effective ministry to men. It is a valuable guide for moving from burned pancakes to disciplemaking.

LEN RUFFNER, *National Director,*
Christian & Missionary Alliance Men's Ministry

Many of us Montana share the vision of using Man in the Mirror to bring a credible message of Jesus to all the men in our state. Discipleship is not easy. Jesus never said it would be. No Man Left Behind provides us with many needed tools to work with. It is exactly what we need.

HARRISON FAGG, *Montana Man in the Mirror*

As the men of the church go, so goes the church. Most Christian denominations in America and Europe are in a serious decline. Men are absent and too many of those in the pews are sadly living as cultural Christians. No Man Left Behind holds the promise of being one of the seminal books of our time for the renewal and revival of Christian men, and for the Kingdom.

DAVID R. REED, *Member, Board of Directors, United Methodist Men's Foundation.*

NO MAN LEFT BEHIND

How to Build and Sustain
a Thriving Disciple-Making Ministry
for Every Man in Your Church

Patrick Morley,
David Delk, and Brett Clemmer

MOODY PUBLISHERS
CHICAGO

All Scripture quotations, unless otherwise indicated, are taken from the *Holy Bible, New International Version.*® NIV.® Copyright © 1973, 1978, 1984 by International Bible Society. Used by permission of Zondervan Publishing House. All rights reserved.

Scripture quotations marked NLT are taken from the *Holy Bible, New Living Translation*, copyright © 1996. Used by permission of Tyndale House Publishers, Inc., Wheaton, Illinois 60189. All rights reserved.

Scripture quotations marked TLB are taken from *The Living Bible* copyright © 1971. Used by permission of Tyndale House Publishers, Inc., Wheaton, Illinois 60189. All rights reserved.

Cover and Interior Design: Smartt Guys design
Cover Image: Joshua Blake
Author photographer: Tim Tew
Editor: Jim Vincent

We hope you enjoy this book from Moody Publishers. Our goal is to provide high-quality, thought-provoking books and products that connect truth to your real needs and challenges. For more information on other books and products written and produced from a biblical perspective, go to www.moodypublishers.com or write to:

Moody Publishers
820 N. LaSalle Boulevard
Chicago, IL 60610

ISBN: 0-8024-7549-3
ISBN-13: 978-0-8024-7549-7

9 10 8

Printed in the United States of America

Library of Congress Cataloging-in-Publication Data

Morley, Patrick M.
    No man left behind : how to build and sustain a thriving disciple-making ministry for every man in your church / Patrick Morley, David Delk, and Brett Clemmer.
        p. cm.
    Includes bibliographical references.
    ISBN-13: 978-0-8024-7549-7
1. Church work with men. 2. Discipling (Christianity) 3. Spiritual formation. I. Delk, David. II. Clemmer, Brett. III. Title.
    BV4440.M67 2006
    259.081--dc22
                                                        2006011805

CONTENTS

ACKNOWLEDGMENTS

THIS BOOK would not have been possible without the collected contributions of thousands of leaders who are striving to disciple men all across the world. Most of what you will read in this book has been learned from these brothers and sisters in the battle for men's souls.

Over one thousand leaders have come through the Leadership Training Center courses held in Orlando, around the United States, and in Asia. These leaders have challenged, encouraged, and inspired us with both their insights and their passion for reaching and discipling men in the local church.

Hundreds of leaders have been involved in the National Coalition of Men's Ministries (NCMM) in its ten-year history, and we have gleaned and benefited much from their collected wisdom and experience. Thanks especially to past and current members of the steering committee, including: Allen Abbott, Leonard Albert, Chuck Brewster, Paul Cole, Vince D'Acchioli, Brian Doyle, Phil Downer, Dan Erickson, Terry Etter, Leary Gates, Geoff Gorsuch, Randy Grubb, Jack Kelley, Rick Kingham, Larry Kreider, Larry Malone, Curt Miller, Ron Roberts, Dr. Dale Schlafer, Chuck Stecker, Chris Van Brocklin, Glen Wagner, and Sid Woodruff. NCMM members are continually looking for new and more effective ways to reach and disciple men through their organizations and denominations.

We would also like to acknowledge our forerunners, like CBMC, which has been in continual existence for seventy-five years; Gene Getz ,who was an early writer to men; Ed Cole and the Christian Men's Network, who pioneered today's movement; and the North American Conference of Church Men's Staff who have gathered for many decades to represent denominational efforts to disciple men.

The staff at Man in the Mirror is simply as fine a collection of individuals as work in any corporation today. Thank you so much to Pam Adkins, Zuleida Aleman, Christina Angelakos, Jim Angelakos, Lucy Blair, Michael Bloomer, Jenny Cameron, Sharon Carey, Stephanie Carter, Bernie Clark, Corrie Cochran, Tracy Dickerhoff, Betty Feiler, Kevin Fittro, Tom Hingle, Joanne Hunt, Jessica Lane, Michael Lenahan, Liz Luke, Michael Maine, Daphne Mayer, Whitney Mayer, Kelly O'Byrne, Dennis Puleo, Thea Risa, Tracie Searles, Antonio Stevens, and Svana Toll. This group of people, working in a little office in a suburb of Orlando, Florida, has impacted more than seven million people in the last twelve years.

We would also like to thank all the folks at Moody Publishers, including Dave DeWit, John Hinkley, Paul Santhouse, Greg Thornton, and Jim Vincent, and the design team at the Puckett Group.

Finally, thanks to our literary agent, Robert Wolgemuth, for his wisdom, patience, and keen sense of what to do next. Thanks for being our wise counselor, fellow visionary, and good friend.

A PASSION FOR NO MAN BEING LEFT BEHIND

FOR TWO DECADES the motto of Brett's pastor, Pete Alwinson, has been, *No Man Left Behind*. So how has it turned out? Of the men attending Pete's church, 95 percent profess faith in Christ, 75 percent are engaged in spiritual growth, and 75 percent are serving the Lord. Those are encouraging results! So when Brett suggested *No Man Left Behind* as the title for this book, we couldn't resist.

We believe nothing has the power to transform the world more than discipling men. We've seen it in churches where leaders like Pete passionately commit to reach all of their men. It's not easy, but it's among a handful of the most important tasks in the world.

On the inside front cover of this book is an image of *The No Man Left Behind Model*. We'll explain this system throughout the book, and our hope is that by the end you will be able to pass the *napkin test*: to explain this system in a few minutes to another man using nothing but a pen and a paper napkin.

This book represents what we have learned in a combined sixty years of experience discipling men, and almost thirty years of working with church leaders who are discipling men. We have worked with churches from more than one hundred denominations, and our organization, Man in the Mirror, has partnerships with more than a dozen denominations. We have conducted more than fifty classes in men's discipleship through our Leadership Training Center. We have worked directly with the leadership teams of more than 2,500 churches, and have had the opportunity to learn from thousands more. We have conducted extensive research and fieldwork in hundreds of churches. We believe God has given us these unique opportunities in large measure so that we would write this book.

This is our life's work. Helping church leaders disciple men is what we do. We have the privilege of waking up every day focused on how to disciple men in the church—*your* church. We will be honored if God uses this book to make your efforts more effective and your path a little easier.

Unless otherwise noted, the stories in this book are true (though names are often disguised). These are real churches and real men with real stories. Each chapter also contains discussion questions and exercises. It will be best if you do these as a team or with another man from your church. The first chapter gives you a helicopter view of the book. The final chapter ties all your work together and helps you outline concrete next steps to more effectively disciple the men of your church.

Thanks for making the investment in this book and in your men. We want to be involved with you and help however we can. We also want to keep learning. If you have questions or feedback, please e-mail us at: nomanleftbehind@maninthemirror.org.

God, as we start this journey we commit ourselves to You. Help us be faithful. Make us passionate for You and for our men. Give us the insights and strategies we need to raise up an army of men who will fight for Your kingdom and glory. In the powerful name of Jesus, amen.

1

MEN'S MINISTRY
IS ROCKET SCIENCE

*Pat has a favorite business saying he picked up somewhere along the way, "Anyone
can bring me a problem; I'm looking for people who can also bring me a solution."
This chapter provides an overview of a proven system to help you disciple every
man in your church. The rest of the book will unpack this system in detail.*

DURING A HIGH-TECH BOOM, a few young professionals in Orlando, Florida,
were creating a dream company. With backgrounds in helping the homeless, the jobless, the disadvantaged, and the sick, they created a unique com-
puterized system to track cases as they passed through the social services
community.

As word got out about this new technology, inquiries poured in from
all over the country. Soon they had a for-profit company, investors, and con-
sultants. They were going to do good in the world. In the process, they
hoped to do well for themselves too.

THE AMERICAN DREAM

Brett was one of the dreamers. In the company's first year, they did their
first million dollars in sales. It was hard work. One person was responsible
for selling the software—Brett. He would go anywhere, anytime, to talk to
anybody. Brett attended countless conferences and made dozens of sales
presentations. He was living the American Dream: being in on the ground
floor of a technology company.

Soon, venture capitalists started calling. They told Brett and his team
how they should grow. They said if certain benchmarks were hit, they

would be ready to invest. Brett and his team began to believe they would hit it big.

Following the venture capitalists' advice, Brett hired a national sales force. Soon six people scattered across the country were looking for potential customers. But those salespeople were new to both social services and the technology, so after they found the prospects, Brett flew out to make the presentations. Instead of one person scheduling trips for him, Brett now had six people doing it!

THE BUBBLE BURSTS

Then the stock market started to go south. Suddenly, the venture capitalists who had been breathlessly waiting for the company to grow stopped returning phone calls—even as Brett and his team met the potential investors' benchmarks.

"When the going gets tough, the tough get going," Brett had heard all his life. So he worked even harder. Even without the capital from those investors, he was determined to make the company a success through sheer will.

One afternoon, Brett got an excited call from his representative in Texas. He asked Brett to come the next day to meet with a large government prospect. A little weary, Brett called his wife, Kimberly, to break the news. He told her he had to go on another trip, and on short notice. Kimberly's response caught him off guard. "That's OK," she said. "It's easier when you're not here."

Brett tried to laugh it off. "Easier when I'm not there. Ha!" He and his wife had two small children, were active in their church, and owned a home. What was she talking about? So when Brett got home, he asked her.

"I mean it's easier when you're not here," she repeated. "You're trying to build a company, I understand. But it's not easy for me either. You call at 5:30 to say you're finishing up and you'll be home in thirty minutes, then you walk in at 8:00. I try to keep dinner warm, but it's ruined. I'm the one who has to answer the kids when they ask, 'Where's Daddy?' or 'Why is Daddy so grumpy?' When you are here, you're so tired that you pretty much ignore us. So go on your trip. We'll be fine. Really. It's just easier when you're not here."

Brett was in trouble. Worst of all, he didn't really know how it happened. He had told himself he was doing it all for his family. He would buy a nice house in a good neighborhood for his wife; send his kids to good schools; give money to charity. But somewhere along the line, he had lost his way. He realized it wasn't really about his family; it was about Brett.

Ironically, while he was losing himself in his company, he and his wife were busy at church, where they led worship for several hundred grade school children in multiple services every weekend.

How did this happen? Brett grew up in church. Now he was a leader in his present church! And yet his wife and family preferred for him to be gone. It was easier. He had become a distraction in their lives.

Why was Brett being left behind? Why hadn't he connected with his church in a way that helped him become a passionate disciple of Jesus Christ?

THE PARADOX OF MEN'S MINISTRY: IT IS ROCKET SCIENCE

Men's Ministry. How hard can it really be? Think about it: You've got men; you've got a church. Add a testimony, some pancakes, a prayer, and—poof!—a men's ministry, right?

Man in the Mirror has worked with thousands of churches across America to help them disciple men. Leaders from churches all over the world have journeyed to Orlando to attend classes at our Leadership Training Center. This book is based on what we've learned from these and other churches. You get to stand on their shoulders.

To encourage and motivate these leaders, we used to tell them: "Look. What we're trying to do here is not rocket science."

And then during one class . . . a new insight. As we stared at this group of leaders struggling to reach men in their churches, we realized these were not clueless men. Many were successful businessmen and leaders in their churches. They were accomplished, intelligent, hardworking men. And yet, year after year they were struggling to reach and disciple their men.

Why? Because men's ministry is just grueling. As one of our leaders has said, "A man is a hard thing to reach."

Men's ministry actually is rocket science. While the process is simple enough, men themselves are quite complex.

When you are working on rockets, things are pretty objective. It's all about physical laws and mathematical concepts like gravity, velocity, angles of ascent, and coefficients of drag. But men are not nearly as predictable. Rockets don't get laid off, have trouble with their kids, or endure a health crisis.

Still, there are some parallels between rocket science and men's ministry. For example:

- *Gravity.* Most men shoulder the burden of supporting a family financially, trying to be a good husband and father, and resisting the temptations of a world that wants to drag them down.
- *Velocity.* New Christians go like gangbusters; but many men have been in church for a long time, and their enthusiasm is waning.
- *Angles of ascent.* Some men get it and steadily move forward; others careen back and forth in their spiritual journey, veering off and hurting people as they go. The key is to ensure they are moving toward Christlikeness.
- *Coefficients of drag.* Jobs, soccer games, family problems, church commitments, hobbies . . . All of these seem to hold men back—leaders too—as they seek to develop their faith and their ministry.

If you've been struggling to get traction in your men's ministry, this should bring you relief and hope. It brings relief when you understand it's not just you (it really is hard to reach and disciple men), and hope because this book contains a strategy that can help you do it. You can reach men in your church. You can get them to grow closer to Christ. This book will show you how.

THE PHYSICS OF MEN'S MINISTRY

You must accept several constants, however, if you are going to launch and sustain a powerful men's ministry. (These will come up again later, but it's good to manage your expectations from the start.) Here are three realistic parameters to remember:

First, it takes a long time to make a disciple. Jesus spent three years with His disciples, traveling with them, eating with them, teaching them. Even then, one of them sold Him out, another one denied he even knew Him, and all of them panicked and hid after Jesus was killed. How can we expect to make disciples in a twenty-four-week class? The corollary to this is . . .

Second, it can take up to ten years to build and sustain a successful men's ministry. That's right. Ten years. As Richard Foster said, "Our tendency is to overestimate what we can accomplish in one year, but underestimate what we can accomplish in ten years."[1] There's just no such thing as an "overnight men's ministry success story." If you stick with it, eventually you'll look around your church and see men who are disciples and leaders. You'll realize that your ministry is responsible in some way for most of those men. And it will take ten years. You are not called to produce immediate results, just to be faithful.

Third, there are no "Five Easy Steps to an Effective Men's Ministry." There aren't even five hard steps. At the Leadership Training Center we sometimes refer to this as "Insert Tab A into Slot B Men's Ministry." It just doesn't work that way. This book is *preceptive,* not *prescriptive.* We explain "why" and "how" to disciple men, but we don't specify exactly "what" you should do. Instead, we will help you plan your own concrete next steps according to the culture and needs of your church.

FROM PROTOTYPE TO MANUFACTURING

The hard, cold reality is that we will not see a revival in America and the world if effective disciple-building of men in churches does not move from the prototype stage to the manufacturing stage. What do we mean by that?

Imagine you were alive in 1900. You might have seen an automobile drive through town. People would have gathered to point and stare at this unusual new apparatus. But only twenty-five years later, to see an automobile would have been no big deal. Why? Because in 1913 Henry Ford invented the assembly line with a conveyor belt. By 1927 the Ford Motor Company had manufactured fifteen million Model T's! Ford helped move the auto industry from the prototype stage to the manufacturing stage.

> ## THE BIG IDEA
> The discipleship system of your church is perfectly designed to produce the kind of men you have sitting in the pews.

Right now, hundreds of churches are doing a wonderful job discipling men. You may have heard about some of them—we can all point and stare and learn from their success. But there are about 350,000 churches in America. Our passion is to see a dynamic disciple-making ministry to men in hundreds of thousands of churches. Discipling men needs to move from an unusual activity in a few churches to a common characteristic of the life of most churches.

A SYSTEM PERFECTLY DESIGNED

What about your church? In business we have an axiom: "Your system is perfectly designed to produce the results you are getting." Imagine a factory where the front right fender falls off of every third car that rolls off the assembly line. The manufacturing "system" of the factory is perfectly designed to produce cars that have a one in three chance of a fender falling off!

This applies to more than manufacturing processes. The same can be said of ministry systems (or models). In other words, the discipleship "system" of your church is perfectly designed to produce the kind of men you have sitting in the pews (or not sitting in the pews, as the case may be).

HOW THIS BOOK IS STRUCTURED

That's why at Man in the Mirror we focus on helping churches by equipping and training leaders, and that's why we wrote this book. We will present you with a system designed to sustain an effective disciple-making ministry to men in your church. This model has been proven in local churches—it's a system that works, a system that's designed to create passionate disciples.

THE NO MAN LEFT BEHIND MODEL
A System Designed to Produce Passionate Disciples

WIDE - DEEP

MEN WHO NEED CHRIST

MAN — ALL-INCLUSIVE MINISTRY TO MEN — MAN — MAN

DISCIPLE

CREATE
VISION
SUSTAIN — CAPTURE

THE THREE STRANDS OF LEADERSHIP
A MAN CODE
PORTAL PRIORITY

DISCIPLE
DISCIPLE | DISCIPLE
DISCIPLE | DISCIPLE | DISCIPLE

This model demonstrates how to build a "people mover" or "conveyor belt" to disciple men within your church. Just like a moving sidewalk at an airport or an assembly line at Henry Ford's factory, this process helps men get from where they are to where God wants them to be.

The remainder of this chapter presents an overview of the components of the model as well as a preview of what's to come in the rest of the book. We'll take a helicopter view and fly over the major concepts and insights. Don't feel like you have to grasp it all now because the following chapters unpack each aspect step-by-step.

Why are we presenting these items here? It's important to be familiar with all these ideas before discussing each one in detail because together they form an integrated whole. This system is most definitely more than the sum of its parts.

The model—and this book—has three sections. The focus of *Part One: The Promise of Men's Ministry* is to better understand how men are doing, what they need, and how to help them. The focus of *Part Two: The Foundations of Your Ministry to Men* is to understand the building blocks of a sustainable discipleship system in your church. The focus of *Part Three: Executing Your Men's Ministry* is to give you a strategy to disciple every man in your church.

By the end of chapter 12—especially if you work through it with a team—you will create a concrete plan for exactly what to do in your church.

Part one will be explored in chapters 2–4; part two in chapters 5–7; and part three in chapters 8–12. Here's a quick introduction to each.

PART 1: THE PROMISE OF MEN'S MINISTRY: WHAT YOUR CHURCH CAN DO FOR MEN

Before you start building a system, it's a good idea to understand both your starting and ending points. We begin with the men. Exactly what is it we hope to accomplish with them?

The men you are trying to reach are the raw materials of your system. The men in your church and community are the inputs on the left side of the conveyor belt. You will read more about the state of men in America in chapter 2.

Disciples. Your goal is to create an environment that God can use to produce disciples. *Disciples* are men who are called to walk with Christ, equipped to live like Christ, and sent to work for Christ (1 Timothy 3:15–17). These are the *outputs*, or products, of your men's ministry system. Disciples are biblical Christians. Some will become leaders, and some of these leaders will become allies. (Read more about disciples in chapter 3.) What do men look like at each of these stages?

1. ***Biblical Christians.*** These are men who grasp the gospel and are hungry to grow. They have stopped seeking the God they want and have begun to seek the God who is. They understand that change takes place from the inside out. They know from their own experience that Christianity is not about behavior modification; it's about heart transformation. We go into greater detail about biblical Christians in chapter 9.

2. ***Leaders.*** These are men who are beginning to live out of the overflow of their own personal relationship with Jesus. No longer are they concerned only with their walk with God; now they want to do what it takes to help other people grow too. These are the "trustworthy" men who will, in turn, pass what they have learned on to others (2 Timothy 2:2 TLB). Read more about leaders in chapter 6.

3. ***Allies.*** These are men who have become passionately convinced that God can use them and your church to transform the world for His glory. These are the men who become future members of your men's leadership team and fuel growth in your discipleship ministry with men. Pray and focus your energies on creating allies. Read more about allies in chapter 4.

PART 2: THE FOUNDATIONS OF YOUR MINISTRY TO MEN

Three components provide a solid base on which to build your men's ministry—the *Portal Priority* (your philosophy of ministry), a *Man Code* (the environment you create for men), and the *Three Strands of Leadership*.

The Portal Priority. Churches that reach men effectively make discipleship their *portal priority* (see Matthew 28:19). By this we mean that all the other initiatives of the church serve the purpose of discipleship. You cannot produce worshipers by begging men to worship; you can't produce tithers by guilting men to give; you can't create evangelists simply by training men to share. Men will not worship a God they do not know and revere; they won't give to a God they don't love; and they won't share about a God they aren't passionate about. Jesus' model is to produce disciples who worship, disciples who tithe, and disciples who are passionate to share the good news about what He has done for them. We discuss the portal priority in chapter 5.

A Man Code. Churches that effectively disciple men have a strong masculine atmosphere. They create an unwritten "man code" that defines what it means to be a man in their church. New men soak it in from the atmosphere: "To be a man here is to be important and valuable, and also to play a part in what God is doing to transform the world." Sometimes the incredible adventure of following Christ is buried beneath boring bulletin announcements. Make your church a place where men can be men. You'll read more about a man code in chapter 5.

The Three Strands of Leadership. To disciple all the men of your church and community, your conveyor belt will need a strong foundation—leadership. Successful discipleship ministries for men have the active involvement of the senior pastor, a committed leader, and an effective and renewed leadership team—three strands of leadership (like the cord of three strands in Ecclesiastes 4:12). Leadership is explored in chapter 6.

ABOVE THE FOUNDATION: THE PROCESS

On top of this foundation, we will help you build a "conveyor belt"—the process of your men's ministry.

Wide to Deep. Churches that reach men build a system that moves men along the "Wide-to-Deep" continuum. A goal of your church's ministry with men is to take men who don't know Christ (interested in opportunities on the wide side) and move them along to become passionate disciples (invested in ministry on the deep side). Each activity or program in your church will appeal to men who are at different points on the continuum. One role of leadership is to make sure all your leaders are on the same page and that you have the entire continuum covered to help disciple every man.

All-Inclusive. Develop an all-inclusive mind-set by recognizing that everything your church does that touches men is men's ministry. In other words, the size of your men's ministry is equal to the number of men in your church. The traditional definition of men's ministry is only those activities that happen when men are by themselves, such as a Saturday morning breakfast. An all-inclusive ministry disciples men right where they are, maximizing the kingdom impact of every interaction with every man. You have a "men's ministry" with every man in your church—the only question is, "Is it effective or ineffective?"

The wide-to-deep continuum and the all-inclusive ministry are both detailed in chapter 7.

PART 3: PLANNING AND EXECUTING YOUR MEN'S MINISTRY

Once the conveyor belt is built, you need an engine to start it in motion. You'll build and execute your plan with the "Vision-Create-Capture-Sustain" strategy. Implementing this strategy helps move men step-by-step along the continuum to become mature disciples. Here's a brief introduction to each element. (They are described in detail in chapters 8–11, respectively.)

Vision. Churches that produce disciples clearly define and communicate their *vision* in ways that resonate with men. Use a name, slogan, and/or phrase that connect with men at a gut level. In every interaction you have with men, explain clearly and passionately how this event or activity helps fulfill your purpose and brings glory to God.

Create. Create momentum with men by creating *value.* Get a man started in discipleship by helping him take a new step spiritually. Invite him to breakfast, to church, or to a special men's activity. If he says yes, it's because you have given him something he believes will be valuable.

Capture. Capture momentum by giving every man a "right next step" at the time that you create momentum. Use short-term, low-threshold activities that make it easy for a man to keep moving forward. For example, offer a six-week topical study on a commonly felt need, such as money or work. Make sure you capture momentum by asking men for a commitment at the time they most feel the value.

Sustain. Sustain momentum by engaging men in the most effective long-term discipleship processes of your church. As quickly as possible, help men enter into meaningful relationships with other men. Most lasting change takes place in the context of relationships. Sustain change by focusing on the heart rather than allowing men to simply be nice and perform.

Repeat this cycle over and over through your interactions with men and see how God uses it to help men become passionate disciples.

Building Your Plan. This system will work differently in every church. In chapter 12, we walk through the entire model again step-by-step. We give you two sets of exercises—one to work through in the next three months, the other in the next year. This will give you a chance to build a concrete plan that fits *your* church.

What's the result of implementing this system in a local church? You'll be a part of a dynamic church filled with passionate men who live and love like Christ. We have seen this in hundreds of churches across America.

WHY IS THIS SO IMPORTANT?

Many leaders we talk to have expressed astonishment over the statistic from Barna Research that only 4 percent of Americans and 9 percent of born-again Christians hold a biblical worldview.[2]

Given the vast amount of money spent by the church each year—approximately $31 billion in 2001[3] (churches representing 49.4 million members)—one is tempted to ask, "What has the church been making, because it sure doesn't seem like it has been making disciples?"

The consequences are staggering. A whopping 40 percent of the baby buster generation were raised by divorced or separated parents. Now the sins of the fathers are being visited on the next generation: Tonight, 33 percent of America's 72 million children will go to bed in a home without a biological father. And 66 percent of them are not expected to live with both biological parents through age eighteen.[4] We are now bearing the full brunt of our failure to disciple men.

code?

THE OPPORTUNITY: THE MAN COMES AROUND

The story we told at the beginning of this chapter is not an illustration. It's the true account of one of the authors—Brett Clemmer.

About the time his wife told him it was easier when he was gone, Brett got a call from a friend, Kevin. "You know how our wives are meeting in that women's Bible study? Well, I was talking to some of the other husbands. Maybe we should have a guys' group too—if for no other reason than to protect ourselves, because I'm pretty sure they're talking about us." Brett was pretty sure too. He wondered what Kevin had heard about *him*? "Sure," Brett said. "What are we going to study?"

"Remember the book they handed out in church a few weeks ago? Just bring that and we'll see if we want to use it."

Brett brought the book. That group, Brett says, was the beginning of a rebirth of his faith:

"The book was *The Man in the Mirror*. We decided to study it, and it saved my marriage, my family, and in many ways, my life. The book spoke directly to what I was going through—the whole concept of *cultural Christianity* seemed like it was taken right from my experience."

Brett adds the most important part of their study was the half-dozen guys he met—"all of us struggling to be good fathers and husbands, all working too hard and trying to find balance. It gave me brothers. And together, we journeyed toward Christ."

Brett's software company eventually went out of business. "But a funny thing happened as my dream of building a company died," Brett said. "As my career plummeted, my relationship with my wife and my kids soared. And I found new life in my relationships with my brothers and with God. Why? Because someone chose to disciple me."

You have men in your church like Brett. This book has been written to help you reach them and disciple them for their good and the glory of Christ. Thanks for joining the adventure. Together, we can ask God to help us make sure that no man is left behind.

REMEMBER THIS

• Men's ministry actually is rocket science, only harder.

• It takes a long time to make a disciple.

• It can take up to ten years to build a successful men's ministry.

• There's no such thing as "The Five Easy Steps to an Effective Men's Ministry."

• Discipling men needs to go from the prototype stage to the manufacturing stage.

• Your system for building disciples is perfectly designed to produce the men who are sitting in your pews—or not.

• *The No Man Left Behind Model* will help you move men step-by-step toward becoming mature disciples.

TALK ABOUT THIS

Discuss these questions with your leadership team.

1. "Men's ministry actually is rocket science." Do you agree or not, and why? What has been your past experience trying to build a men's ministry?

2. In a few sentences, how would you describe the "system" for reaching and discipling men in your church today? What kind of results have you been getting?

3. Look back at *The No Man Left Behind Model*. Which concepts are you looking forward to learning about, and why?

PRAY ABOUT THIS

Pray together as a leadership team . . .

• that God will unite your hearts as you seek to develop an effective discipleship ministry to men in your church.

• that God will reveal how you can apply what you learn.

• that your church will be a place where every man is discipled and no man is left behind.

PART ONE

THE PROMISE OF MEN'S MINISTRY

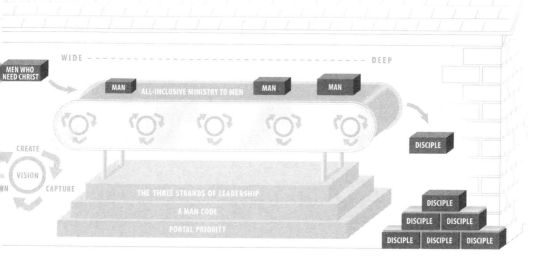

No Man Fails
on Purpose

Before you can get the right answer, you have to ask the right question. What is the state of men in America today? And what difference does it make? When we see and understand the ramifications of men who are failing, we'll understand that starting with men is a systemic solution to the problems of our churches and the world.

MANY, IF NOT MOST, of our cultural problems—divorce, abortion, juvenile crime, fatherlessness—can be traced back to the failure of a man. Ironically, it's a man who got up in the morning hoping to succeed.

The signs are all around us. We live in a country where every third child is born out of wedlock; where 24 million kids don't live with their biological fathers; where about half of all marriages end in divorce. We can read these statistics and just blow by them. Or we can consider what they mean for our country and our churches. Wouldn't you agree that there must be something systemically wrong with a culture that allows these things to happen?

Fatherlessness is a rampant and well-documented problem in our society. Only a third of all children in America will live with both of their biological parents through the age of eighteen. Half of all children in broken homes have not seen

> • **72,000,000** children under eighteen. Tonight, 33 percent of them will go to bed in a home without a biological father.
>
> • **40 percent** of first marriages end in divorce, affecting one million children each year. Divorce rates for second and third marriages are higher.
>
> • **33 percent** of all children are born out of wedlock.
>
> SOURCES: U.S. Census Bureau; Wade F. Horn and Tom Sylvester, *Father Facts*, 4th ed.; (Gaithersburg, MD: National Fatherhood Initiative, 2002); and James Dobson, *Bringing Up Boys* (Wheaton: Tyndale, 2001).

their father in over a year. Children who come from fatherless homes are five times more likely to live in poverty, have emotional problems, and repeat a grade.[1]

Yet, these are all symptoms of deeper systemic issues. Treating symptoms is necessary and good, but you can't cure a disease by treating the symptoms. So while there are many sociological and psychological studies to explain why we have so many problems, the "root" problem—the systemic problem—is that we have not properly discipled our men. The only way to solve systemic problems is with systemic solutions.

BABIES IN THE RIVER

In social service circles, a parable is told about a small village on the edge of a river. One day one of the villagers noticed a baby floating in the water. The villager quickly swam out to save the baby and brought it to shore.

The next day another villager was walking beside the river and saw two babies in the river. He quickly jumped in the water and rescued them. The following day four babies were rescued by the villagers. Every day the number of children in the water increased.

The villagers organized themselves quickly, building piers, tying rope lines, and training teams to rescue babies. They were soon working day and night. And still the number of children floating down the river increased each day.

The villagers worked as hard as they could, even to the point of exhaustion. But no one ever asked the question, "Why are these babies in the river? Let's go upstream and see where they are coming from."

What is the upstream cause of our cultural and spiritual ills? Consider a concrete issue like divorce. You sometimes hear a story about a wife who had an affair and left her husband, or a child whose behavior is so bad it rips the family apart. But you only hear about these stories because they are relatively rare. And often, even if a wife does have an affair, it's only after years of emotional neglect—if not abuse—by a husband *who was never taught what it takes to have a successful marriage.*

Consider teen pregnancy: Young men who have been instilled with the proper values *by their father* will know how to treat young women. Young women who are secure in the love of their father and of God won't look for acceptance in the arms of young men. Do the men in your church know how to teach their teenagers about sex, chastity, and God's plan for them to find happiness in a loving marriage relationship?

How about crime? Men comprise 93 percent of the prison population in America. And of those, 85 percent report having no father figure in their lives.[2] How many of those men would be in jail right now if their fathers had stuck around and been involved in their lives?

No one is trying to beat up on men here. If anything, we're saying: "Look how important men are! Look what happens when they aren't taught to do the right things!"

BUT IT'S BETTER IN THE CHURCH, RIGHT?

You'd think the church would be a safe haven from many of these disturbing statistics. Surely kids who grow up going to church will have a foundation of faith that carries into adulthood. If a couple goes to church together, you would think that their marriage will be much more likely to succeed. Unfortunately, neither of these assumptions is true.

In fact, men in the church face the same challenges and frustrations as men outside of the church. For example, for every ten men in the church:
- Nine will have children who leave the church.[3]
- Eight will not find their jobs satisfying.[4]
- Six will pay the monthly minimum on their credit card bills.[5]
- Five will have a major problem with pornography.[6]
- Four will get divorced—affecting one million children each year.[7]
- Only one will have a biblical worldview.[8]
- All ten will struggle to balance work and family.

Ask pastors to list the problems and struggles their members face. They sound like the chapter headings in a social work textbook: alcohol and substance abuse, domestic violence, juvenile crime, depression, shattered relationships, to name just a few.

What is happening? If most of the major societal problems we face can be traced back to the failure of men, why aren't men in the church doing any better than men outside of the church?

The answer? We are not discipling men to be followers of Jesus Christ. Our churches are not effectively helping men understand what it takes to be a godly husband, a godly father, and a godly man.

The Numbers Aren't Pretty

There are an estimated 113 million men in America fifteen years of age and older.[9] Of those, 69 million—61 percent—make no profession of faith in Jesus Christ whatsoever.[10] Therefore, barely more than a third of the men in America indicate they are followers of Christ.

So is the church doing a good job with the men who are present? Of the 44 million men who profess faith in Christ, only an estimated six million men are involved in any kind of ongoing or intentional discipleship program.[11] That's one in seven of the men who profess faith in Christ, and only one out of eighteen men in America.

APPROXIMATE BREAKDOWN OF AMERICAN MEN BY LEVEL OF SPIRITUAL DEVELOPMENT		
Number of men in U.S. (age 15 and above)	**113 million**	**100%**
Men who make no profession of faith	69 million	61%
Men who profess faith in Christ	44 million	39%
• Not involved in any discipleship process	38 million	33% (of all men)
• Involved in ongoing discipleship in some way	6 million	6% (of all men)

SOURCES: U.S. Census Bureau; The Barna Group: www.barna.org/cgi-bin/PageCategory.asp?CategoryID=19 and www.barna.org/FlexPage.aspx?Page=BarnaUpdate&BarnaUpdateID=61

Figure 1

Imagine taking eighteen men to a baseball field, breaking them up into two teams, and giving them helmets, bats, balls, and gloves. Now imagine that only one of them had ever seen a baseball game. What would happen? It would be chaos! Men would be throwing balls at other men and chasing each other around the field. They would ask questions like, "Why are there three rubber squares and one rubber pentagon?" or, "What's with these huge gloves?!" They just wouldn't get it. That's what is happening in our culture today. Only one out of eighteen men is learning how to be a godly man, so we suffer divorce, fatherlessness, crime, and other societal problems.

START WITH THE MEN

Reducing these ills will not come from social reforms alone. They will come from spiritual reforms. What we need is nothing less than a moral and spiritual reformation of society.

Think about this for a moment: Is there any way we can get society right if we don't first get the church right? If that is true, then is there any way we can get the church right if we don't first get families right? If that is true, is there any way we can get families right, if we don't first get marriages right? And if that is true, is there any way we can get marriages right if we don't get men right?

How then do we get men right? By discipling them to be followers of Jesus Christ! A spiritual reformation of society starts with a spiritual reformation of men.

Can this be done? More importantly, will it work? It has been done before: "For God so loved the world that he gave his one and only Son," Jesus, who gathered around Himself twelve regular men, and together they changed the world.

THE MISSION: OUR MARCHING ORDERS

Matthew 28 contains the single most effective speech ever delivered. More millions of people and billions of dollars have been mobilized by this speech than any other in human history:

> Therefore go and make disciples of all nations, baptizing them in the name of the Father and of the Son and of the Holy Spirit, and teaching them to obey everything I have commanded you. And surely I am with you always, to the very end of the age. *(Matthew 28:19–20)*

Who would have thought this brief speech, given to a ragtag group of men, most of whom had probably never been more than forty-five miles or so from their homes, would have resulted in *billions* of people following Jesus Christ? Who were these guys? They were men just like the ones you have at your church:

*To get **society** right...*

*Get the **church** right; to get the church right,*

*Get **families** right; to get families right,*

*Get **marriages** right; to get marriages right,*

*Get **men** right.*

- some small business owners—Peter, James, and John were fishermen
- a snob—Nathanael, who said "Nazareth! Can anything good come from there?"
- an accountant—Judas Iscariot kept track of the money
- a religious guy—Simon the Zealot
- a government employee—Matthew, the tax collector
- young guys—Andrew, and maybe all of them, were in their early twenties or even younger

THE BIG IDEA

A spiritual reformation of society starts with a spiritual reformation of men.

Jesus discipled these men and they changed the world. If you will disciple the men of your church to follow Christ, what will happen? Marriages will improve, then families, then the church, and finally the world.

The church is already lacking men. In the average church in America, there are three women for every two men.[12] Think about it: Why would God give our churches more men when we are doing such an inadequate job of discipling the ones we already have? And why would a man want to go to a church where the men he sees look almost identical to the ones who don't go?

We need to start with men. They need to be discipled. If they aren't, they will eventually find something else to hold their attention.

THE STAKES: A PERSONAL STORY

It's a story that we hear too often. In fact, Pat has lived it. His dad, Bob, was abandoned by his father when he was two years old. Bob and his three siblings were raised by a single mom. "She did a great job. But my father never felt the scratch of his dad's whiskers, never smelled his work clothes, never heard him whistle while he worked, never heard him read a bedtime story, never watched how he did chores. My father never saw his own dad wink at his mom, never heard him say, 'I love you, son' or 'I'm proud of you, son.' Without a dad he had to 'guess' at what it meant to be a man, husband, and a father to me."

When Bob turned six, he went to work with his older brother, Harry, on a bread truck and paper route before school. They got up at 3:00 a.m. and had a permanent tardy slip to school. When a man fails he doesn't just ruin his own life, he usually takes down a good woman and two, three, or four children with him.

"When my dad became an adult, he had to decide if he would repeat the sins of his father or break the cycle. He really wanted to break the cycle," Pat recalls. "So when Dad had four boys of his own, our family joined a church for help. Unfortunately, our church had a vision to put my dad to work, but no vision to disciple him to be a godly man, husband, and father. As a result, my dad became successful as a worker, but as a disciple he got left behind. So, at the age of forty, when my dad was the top lay leader in the church (I was in the tenth grade, my younger brothers were in the seventh, fifth, and third grades), he and my mother just got burned out and we left the church.

"The results have been tragic," Pat says. "That single decision put our family into a tailspin from which, over forty years later, we have still not fully recovered: two high school dropouts, drug addiction, alcoholism, employment problems, and divorce. One brother died of a heroin overdose. It has been more than three quarters of a century since my dad was abandoned by his father, and forty years after our family dropped out of church.

"I can't help but wonder how our family would have been different if our church had offered a men's discipleship ministry. I will never know. But I hope the men in your church and their sons and daughters will."

Obviously, Pat will never know, but the men in your church can. Your church can break the cycle. "God brought the gospel into my family line through my wife's family line. My wife led me to Christ and, in turn, I was able to help introduce Dad, Mom, and two brothers to Christ as their Savior. Our two children love Christ and have both married Christians spouses." So, by God's grace, Pat did break the cycle, but it took two generations instead of one.

What was the difference between Pat and his father? Pat got involved in a church that had a vision to disciple him to live like Christ—a church

Q & A

How long did Jesus take to pick His disciples?

You might think that Jesus called each of the Twelve the first time He saw them. Luke 6 indicates that after spending quite some time in ministry with a larger group of followers, Jesus spent *a whole night in prayer*. And in the morning, "He called his disciples to him and chose twelve of them whom he also designated apostles" (verse 13). Jesus invited them into ministry with Him early but it was only after spending time with them—up to two years—and a whole night in prayer that He designated them as part of the inner twelve.

committed to making sure Pat was not left behind.

Pat's dad and mom died in 2002. If his dad were still alive, Pat would say to him, "Dad, I know you wanted to break the cycle. I know that things didn't turn out like you dreamed. But Dad, we have broken the cycle. Sure, it took two generations instead of one. But God has done it."

Pat knows that if his dad were still alive, Bob would say, "I am responsible for taking us out of church." That's admirable. However, the church must also accept culpability. As a church, they had a vision for putting Bob to work, but they didn't have a vision for helping him become a disciple.

No More Men Left Behind

Pat's dad was a good man. He didn't want to fail. If he could have seen what was coming around the bend, he would have made a different decision. He never saw it coming. The church, on the other hand, should have seen it coming. It's time to fix this system so that future generations of men become disciples and don't get left behind.

You probably have a man in your church just like Pat's dad—trying to be a good man, full of good intentions, full of hopes and dreams for his family, a man who wants to break the cycle. He is a man looking to you for guidance. His sons and daughters may be in your nursery or youth group, and they have no idea what is about to happen when Dad leaves the church. Please, for the sake of Christ and His kingdom, identify that man and disciple him to be a godly man, husband, and father.

Pat can testify how important this is. His dad's church missed its moment. From that one error his family has suffered needlessly for over forty years. It doesn't have to happen to your men—you can build a system that God can use to disciple every man in your church.

Wanting to do something is not the same as doing it. What kind of men are you trying to make? The next chapter will help you define a disciple so that you can know what you are trying to produce.

REMEMBER THIS

- Many of today's cultural problems can ultimately be traced back to the failure of a man.

- No man fails on purpose.

- Men in the church face the same problems and issues as men outside of the church.

- Only one out of eighteen men in America is actively involved in discipleship.

- Jesus poured His life and ministry into twelve young men. On these men He built the church.

- If you disciple men, marriages will improve, then families, then the church, and finally, the world.

- Our churches need to have a vision for building disciples, not just putting people to work.

TALK ABOUT THIS

1. Are we giving men a bum rap when we say that most of the cultural problems we face can be traced to the failure of a man? Why or why not?

2. Do the women outnumber the men in your church? What is the ratio of men to women? What are some of the reasons for this? What difference will it make?

3. All of us have known men who failed—in their marriage, career, relationships with kids—even though they had no intention of failing. What do you think happened?

4. Estimate the percentage of men in your church actively involved in discipleship. What are some of the opportunities for discipleship that your church offers to men? What are some of the reasons that the men who are involved got involved? What are some of the reasons that the men who are not involved have stayed on the outside?

PRAY ABOUT THIS

Pray together as a leadership team...

- that God will give the leadership of your church a renewed vision for the importance of discipling men.

- that God will work in the lives of specific men you know who are failing in some way—spiritually, emotionally, physically, financially, and relationally.

- that God will continue to bond your hearts together in a shared vision to disciple every man in your church, and that He will call more leaders in your church to this vision.

What Is a Disciple?

At our Leadership Training Center, we commonly hear the question, "What exactly is a disciple?" It's a great question—you have to know what you are trying to produce before you implement a system to produce it! This chapter will discuss the motivations of men, define "disciple," and describe a process by which men become disciples of Jesus Christ.

IN OUR EXPERIENCE with men and men's leaders, we have found three things that every man wants:

- *something* to give their lives to,
- *someone* to share it with, and
- a personal *system* that offers a reasonable explanation for why the first two are so difficult!

This is perfectly illustrated in Ecclesiastes, when Solomon wrote:

There was a man all alone; he had neither son nor brother. There was no end to his toil, yet his eyes were not content with his wealth. "For whom am I toiling," he asked, "and why am I depriving myself of enjoyment?" This too is meaningless—a miserable business! *(Ecclesiastes 4:8)*

What Do Men Want?

All men want something to give their lives to: a mission, a cause, or a purpose. Every man wants to get to the end of his life and feel like it counted for something, like he mattered. For many, like the man in Ecclesiastes, they find this in their work. They want to build a company, a career—or at least a bank account—that others will look at with respect and admiration. For other men it's charitable work, or the homeowners association, or their kids' accomplishments.

The common thread is this: Men want to be involved in something bigger than themselves, something that is meaningful.

In addition to something to give their lives to, men want someone to share their lives with. John Eldredge refers to this as "a beauty to win." Typically it includes marriage, but it goes beyond marriage as well. A man "with neither son nor brother" soon finds his toil is "meaningless." Contrary to popular opinion, men were made for relationships; those relationships just might not look like Oprah thinks they should. How else would we explain the popularity of fraternities, softball teams, and bars? Brett recently went to the gun range with his pastor, and nearly every man who came to shoot came with at least one buddy.

All of us are looking for meaning, happiness, peace, tranquility, contentment. By default, a man will look for satisfaction primarily in his accomplishments (something to give his life to) and in other people (someone to share it with).

But most men will also tell you they are frustrated with the difficulty of finding success in accomplishment and relationships. Most of the "systems" that men buy into seem to answer either one problem or the other: Work as hard as you can to build a successful career, stay late, take on the big projects, travel on a moment's notice. But a system designed to maximize your career will undermine your ability to have meaningful relationships in your life. You might build a prosperous lifestyle, but you will have no one to enjoy it with.

Alternatively, you can build a life that depends on other people. Have you seen the sitcom *Cheers*? Everyone yelled "Norm!" when the lovable accountant strolled into his favorite watering hole. But his dedication to the guys at the bar undermined every other relationship and responsibility in his life.

Every man has to decide what he believes will make him happy. A man who puts his faith in his career or achievements will soon find that the world constantly asks the same question: "What have you done for me lately?" Fail to perform and the party's over. A man who puts his faith in relationships with others will find that his friends—or even his wife—are his best buddies until he puts his own needs in front of theirs. It's a variation on the same theme. At some point the man will decide he needs a new job, new friends, or a new wife. Eventually he will say, "This too is meaningless—a miserable business!"

WHAT DO MEN NEED?

The obvious answer to the question "What do men need?" is that they need the gospel. The gospel is the one system that really works—a system that *helps men change the core affections of their hearts.*

The most important thing we can do is to let men know that there is a system that explains why it is so hard to find happiness in achievement or relationships in this world. We have a system that shows them what authentic happiness is and how they can achieve it. It's called the gospel, and it's all explained in the Bible.

This process of helping men move from relying on themselves or others to relying on God is *discipleship.* As the model shows, it is a process of deepening a man's relationship with God. But just exactly what does it mean to be a "disciple"?

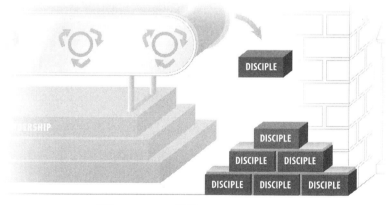

"DISCIPLE" DEFINED

In the Bible, the word for *disciple* literally means "pupil" or "learner." When applied to the early Christians, it came to mean someone who declared a personal allegiance to the teachings and person of Jesus. Today, the life of a disciple revolves around Jesus.

43

We would like to suggest *three conditions* that, if met, qualify a person to be counted as a disciple. (All three conditions must be present. Further, if these three conditions are met, the person should not claim to *not* be a disciple.)

* First, a disciple is called to walk with Christ; they profess faith in Jesus Christ.
* Second, a disciple is equipped to live like Christ; they are engaged in a process of spiritual growth and transformation.
* Third, a disciple is sent to work for Christ; they serve the Lord.

The biblical case for this definition can be made by examining Paul's admonition to Timothy in 2 Timothy 3:15–17:

> From infancy you have known the holy Scriptures, which are able to make you wise for salvation through faith in Christ Jesus. *[Calling]*
> All Scripture is God-breathed and is useful for teaching, rebuking, correcting and training in righteousness, *[Equipping]*
> so that the man of God may be thoroughly equipped for every good work. *[Sending]*

First and foremost, a disciple is someone who has believed in Jesus—His life, work, death, and resurrection. The first task of making disciples is *evangelism*—to call men to walk with Christ by grace through faith.

A lot of people who reject Christianity see Christians and say, "If that's what it means to be a Christian, then I want no part of it." Isn't that a criticism too dangerous to leave unanswered? It may do more harm than good to invite a man to become a Christian if we have no plan to help him truly know and follow Christ.

THE BIG IDEA

A disciple is called to walk with Christ, equipped to live like Christ, and sent to work for Christ.

The second task of making disciples is *teaching*—to equip them to live like Christ. When we don't disciple (train and equip) a man who professes Christ, he will almost always become lukewarm in faith, worldly in behavior, and hypocritical in witness.

Why do we equip men to live like Christ? So they can enjoy Christ by knowing Him better, but also "so that the man of God may be thoroughly equipped for every good work" (2 Timothy 3:16–17). Jesus prayed, "As the Father has sent me, I am sending you" (John 20:21).

Every man wants to give his life to a cause, to make a difference, to do something with his life. When we disciple a man, he will eventually want to make that difference for the glory of God: to "bear much fruit" and do good works "that will last" (John 15:8, 16).

The third task of making disciples is moving men toward *service* and *missions*—sending men to work for Christ, to build His kingdom and bring Him glory. Once a man has been with Christ, experienced the joy of His grace, the warmth of His love, the cleansing of His forgiveness, and the indwelling of His Spirit, he inevitably comes to a point when he can no longer be happy unless he is serving the Lord.

HEAD, HANDS, HEART

A man is not a mature disciple until the truth is understood, believed, and lived out. Use the key words "head," "heart," and "hands" to remember these three concepts.

Head

Men must first understand the truth of the gospel. They need to grow in their knowledge of God's character and how He wants them to live.

Sometimes, a church puts too much emphasis on head knowledge. Basically, every event offered by their ministry has a teaching focus. In this case, we reproduce men with "big heads" but very small hearts and hands.

Heart

Men need to have a growing conviction that the gospel is true and that God can be trusted. Along with knowledge, they need an emotional connection to Christ. Their worldview needs to shift so that they begin to see things from a godly perspective.

Sometimes, a men's ministry can put too much emphasis on emotion. In this case, men can come to God mainly for an emotional "fix." Instead of serving God with all of their lives, they base their Christian experience mainly on their feelings.

Hands

To really understand the truth at the deepest level, you have to put it into practice. It would be unlikely that we really understood Jesus' teaching about the poor until we do something to help a poor person. We must always strive to give men the opportunity to live out what they are learning through our ministry.

 Sometimes though, we can put too much emphasis on performance or duty. In this case, men will define Christianity mainly in terms of whether they fulfilled a certain set of rules or expectations. This easily becomes a "works-based" righteousness that will eventually alienate a person from God and His grace.

In your ministry to men, strive for a balanced approach so that men learn the truth at all three of these levels. Next, what are the methods your church can use to actually make disciples?

HOW DO YOU MAKE A DISCIPLE?

Many methods come to mind, but *the best methods for making disciples are the ones you will use.* Which of these are most suitable for you?

Preaching and Teaching

The age-old starting point for making disciples is the preaching and teaching of God's Word. Don't underestimate the power of the preached Word. God has called some to be pastors and teachers "to equip God's people to do his work and build up the church, the body of Christ" (Ephesians 4:12 NLT). Pastors, make sure your people walk out thinking, "Isn't God awesome!"

Small Groups

A man read *The Man in the Mirror* and accepted the challenge to start an accountability group. That group grew to eight men, then split into four groups. Two of the men approached the pastor to start a men's ministry. After seven years, about seventy-five other groups existed with an estimated nine hundred men. Small groups are a dynamic way to build disciples.

What kinds of small groups are there?

- Bible studies
- accountability groups
- prayer groups
- share groups
- groups for men only
- couples groups
- home groups
- office groups

Most meaningful change takes place in the context of small-group relationships. As men tell their "stories," the truth of the gospel gets meaty and fleshy. Simply, we just "get it" (the gospel) better when we see it in your life!

Private Study

Do your men lack power? Jesus said, "Your problem is that you don't know the Scriptures, and you don't know the power of God" (Matthew 22:29 NLT). Men become disciples when they discover God in His Word. Personally, we have never known a single man whose life has changed in any significant way apart from the regular study of God's Word. For the last two decades, Pat has read *The One Year Bible* through each year. He is convinced this is why he is still walking closely with Christ.

Encourage men to use private study time to memorize meaningful verses, pray, sing, and meditate on God's Word.

Christian Literature

In 1656, Puritan Richard Baxter said, "See that in every family there are some useful moving books, beside the Bible. If they have none, persuade them to buy some: if they be not able to buy them, give them some if you can. If you are not able yourself, get some gentlemen, or other rich persons, that are ready to do good works, to do it."[1] We see it over and over . . . a man will get hold of a book, and God will use the book to get hold of the man. Give a guy a book!

Q & A

How do some men always seem to have the right verse or passage whenever they need it?

Many men who do this have something in common. It's not a photographic memory. It's journaling. Try keeping a small notebook beside you and jot down notes and reflections whenever you read the Bible or a Christian book. Also consider memorizing Scriptures that have made an impact on you (Psalm 119:9, 11).

Seminars and Conferences

A man said, "Wow, that seminar changed my life!" This was quite discouraging to his pastor. He thought, *That speaker didn't say anything to my men that I haven't been saying for years!* And he's right! God can only reap through a seminar in proportion to what the pastor has sown through his weekly work. So the seminar speaker reaps where another has sown. Both, then, should give all glory to God for what God has done (John 4:36). Seminars and conferences do change men's lives.

Informal Discussions

Some of the richest times of our lives are found "hanging out" with buddies. Going to lunch, riding motorcycles, talking theology with friends—God often orchestrates teachable moments to build into each other's lives.

Leadership Training

Pat's father-in-law says, "Amateurs teach amateurs to be amateurs." We agree. If you are serious about making disciples, you really should get some training.

All of these activities can help a man know Christ, but how will you offer them strategically? How can you make sure they are more than a set of hoops that a man jumps through to justify himself before God? In the next chapter we will look at how men change and how God can use your system to change their hearts.

REMEMBER THIS

- Every man wants three things: *something* to give his life to; *someone* to share it with; and a *system* that gives a reasonable explanation for why the first two are so difficult.

- Men often look for success in accomplishments and relationships.

- Every man needs a system that helps him change the core affections of his heart—the gospel.

- A disciple is someone who is called to walk with Christ, equipped to live like Christ, and sent to work for Christ (see 2 Timothy 3:15–17).

- We make disciples by evangelizing, teaching, and providing opportunities to serve.

- A mature disciple understands, believes, and lives out the truth of the gospel with his head, hands, and heart.

- There are many methods to make disciples—most of which your church is probably already doing.

TALK ABOUT THIS

1. What are some examples of how men seek a sense of purpose and significance? In what ways—righteously or sinfully—do men seek "someone" to share their lives with?

2. What are some of the "systems" men you know use to explain life? What difference does this make in their life?

3. How have you seen the gospel change a man's heart in your church or community? Share what happened and how it impacted you.

PRAY ABOUT THIS

Pray together as a leadership team . . .

- that men in your church and community would turn to Christ to find a sense of purpose, significance, and fulfillment.

- that God would engage men's hearts, minds, souls, and strength in drawing them closer to Himself and give them a vision for building His kingdom.

How Do Men Change? Helping Men Experience Heart Transformation

In the previous chapters we gave you some tools to define what a disciple looks like. It would be natural for you to ask, "How does a man become one?" This chapter helps you understand how a man changes and why your ministry should focus on helping men change the core affections of their hearts. You can create a wonderful discipleship system, but if you leave men to themselves, they will simply go through the motions. Pay close attention to this chapter so your ministry won't lack the power to truly transform men's lives.

A LEADER TOLD US the story of "Lou," a man he met in a small group shortly after joining their church. Lou and his wife had been in the church for more than fifteen years. He had been a deacon for a time. He had a wonderful wife; his kids were active in the church. On the outside, everything looked great. A few months of sitting in the small group did nothing to change anyone's opinion. Lou didn't speak out a lot, but when he did, it was worth listening to.

One day, this man got a call from Lou's small-group leader. Lou had left his wife and kids. He had been having an affair for several months, and was taking some time to "figure out what he wanted to do." He never came back.

How can this happen? How can a man sit in a small group, serve as a deacon in his church, seem like the great father in a great family, and then one day just chuck it all?

MEN IN AMERICA: THE STRUGGLE OF SELF-RELIANCE

In Habakkuk, God describes the Babylonian army that is threatening Jerusalem:

> They are a feared and dreaded people; they are a law to themselves and promote their own honor. . . . Then they sweep past like the wind and go on—guilty men, whose own strength is their god. (*Habakkuk 1:7, 11*)

God says the Babylonians are "a law to themselves" (they do whatever they want), they "promote their own honor" (they look out for number one), and their "own strength is their God" (they rely on themselves). Sounds like many men today.

This is our fundamental struggle. Every moment of every day we choose either to live out of our own strength and be independent from God, or to depend on God alone and walk by faith. When we try to be independent, we sin. When we walk by faith, Christ's righteousness is lived out in obedience.

The system of this world is almost perfectly designed to encourage our men to rely on their own strength. It is easy for our projects and pressures to become more real to us than Jesus. Instead of walking by faith, we let our strength become our god. Then we become controlling, angry, panicked, bitter, defensive, proud, and withdrawn.

Performance Versus Faith

How are men successful in the world? We quickly figure out that we have to dress a certain way, have a certain job, make a certain amount of money, live in the right house, or have a good family. The focus is on external things that we can do or see.

So we take a man from this world's system and plop him down in church. He wants to be a "successful Christian." He looks around and decides he needs to dress a certain way, use certain phrases, attend church a certain number of times, give money, serve on committees, and join a men's class. Often we take a man from one performance-oriented culture (the world) and move him right into another one (the church).

In both of these scenarios a man is basically relying on his own strength to be his god. We end up with men who are focused on whether their external behavior matches some ideal, but who are disconnected from a heart of faith.

Men know how to play the game, and, if you let them, they will follow your rules to perfection. The only problem is that in ten or twenty years, like Lou, they will realize that their hearts are dead.

Why Is This So Important?

Would you say the following statement is true or false (go with your first reaction): "Every man does exactly what he wants to do"?

It's actually somewhat of a trick question, since it depends on how you define the word *want*.

In what sense is this statement false? Every man has good intentions on which he doesn't follow through—that's why the price of health club memberships rises in January and goes on sale in March. And men often conform to others' expectations rather than behaving how they might otherwise. Paul himself said, "I do not understand what I do. For what I want to do I do not do, but what I hate I do" (Romans 7:15).

Yet there is also a profound sense in which this statement is true. At the moment of decision, a man chooses to do one thing over another. Even when facing outside pressure or temptation, he evaluates the pros and cons and chooses what he believes will bring the greatest happiness. Whether a man gives in to lust and views pornography on the Internet or sacrificially loves his wife and hangs the curtains, he makes choices based on his worldview and beliefs. Actions are the last step in a process that starts with our attitudes, faith, and desires.

Pascal said it this way: "Happiness is the motive of every action of every man, even of those who hang themselves." Jonathan Edwards said, "The will is the mind choosing."

Jesus too makes it clear that what we do comes from our hearts. He says that "out of the overflow of the heart the mouth speaks" (Matthew 12:34) and indicates a good tree brings forth good fruit, but a bad tree brings forth bad fruit (see verse 35).

He makes this even more explicit in Matthew 15:18–20. Jesus says "The things that come out of the mouth come from the heart, and these make a man 'unclean.' For out of the heart come evil thoughts, murder, adultery, sexual immorality, theft, false testimony, slander. These are what make a man 'unclean.'" The external actions of a man are motivated by his worldview and beliefs.

> We must get beyond a performance orientation. A man's actions will eventually reflect what is happening in his heart. Just like you can't treat cancer by putting a Band-Aid on a man's skin, you can't help a man become a disciple by fixing his behavior and allowing him to ignore his heart. *Christianity is not about behavior modification; it's about heart transformation.*

You have no doubt known men like Lou. They learn to look like a man who is walking with Christ, but their hearts are not being transformed

THE **BIG** IDEA

Christianity is not about behavior modification; it's about heart transformation.

from the inside out. After years of conforming to other people's expectations, a temptation or crisis comes along and they decide to do what they really want to do. Like Bill Murray's character in the movie *Groundhog Day*, they finally say, "I'm not going to live by their rules anymore." And so what was buried in their hearts is revealed when they walk away from Christ.

CREATING AN ENVIRONMENT GOD CAN USE TO CHANGE MEN'S HEARTS

How can you keep this from happening to your men? Many churches rely heavily on information to help men become disciples. Men need to know the truth, but head knowledge is not enough to change a heart. For instance, every person who smokes in America knows smoking causes cancer, yet most continue to smoke.

What kinds of things does God typically use to touch a man's heart? Consider your own life. What is one of the most moving experiences you've had in the last few months? When was the last time you cried other than because of grief? What has God used to move you forward in your relationship with Him?

When we ask these questions about what moves us at our Leadership Training Center, here are some of the answers we receive:

- *Prayer.* God often uses times of prayer—especially being prayed for—to touch a man's heart. Talking to God and listening for His voice cause men to become open to being transformed by the Holy Spirit. Help men enter into times of prayer with and for one another. Easily the richest times at our Leadership Training Center courses are when the leaders share their needs and pray for one another.
- *Music.* One of our faculty members spoke at a men's event one time where a young woman sang a song about a father. It included a verse that told of a young girl who got out of bed late at night and saw her father looking at pornography on a computer. When she was finished singing, there wasn't a dry eye in the room. God used that song in a way that was different than anything else accomplished through the rest of the seminar.
- *Drama/film clips.* All of us have been moved by particularly poignant scenes from movies or plays. Use high-quality drama to help men get out of their normal way of thinking.
- *Testimonies and stories.* Men connect with stories. You probably know a man in your church whose story has been a tremendous encouragement to you. Help men learn to share their experiences and give them a venue to hear what God is doing in the lives of others.
- *Activities.* If you're like most men, you vividly remember a conversation you had with a man while fishing or throwing the football. God wired men for movement, tasks, and activities. Get men moving so God can touch their hearts.
- *Shared experiences.* God uses trials, challenges, and adventure to bond men to one another. Does your ministry get men into situations where they can relate and rely on one another? Competition, service projects, mission trips, or working together on a ministry team for the church—all these things help men reach a new level of brotherhood.
- *Relationships.* Most of what it means to be a disciple is caught, not taught. Men's hearts change as they "do life" together with other men. Consider your own life; much of what you know about being a man was probably learned from other men who invested in your life.
- *Children.* Men get emotional about their kids. Find ways to connect them with their children and other children who need help. Early in his marriage, Pat joined a parenting class at church that began with a

family outing. Without telling the class members what he was doing, the teacher took pictures of all the children at the event. The next Sunday, the teacher began the class with a slide show of the children to the song "Cat's in the Cradle." Pat still remembers the moment more than twenty years later.

- *Service to others.* Men find a deep and lasting joy when they get out of their comfort zones and serve other people. And a disciple is sent to work for Christ. Find ways to get as many men as possible into some kind of meaningful service to people who need to see the love of Christ in action.
- *A man committed to him.* Many men have no real friends. Yet all men need someone who truly wants the best for them. God often uses relationships to change a man's heart.

Are you building these kinds of things into your men's discipleship system? Make a concerted effort to do more than just make sure men are in the right classes or groups—create an environment where God can work to change their hearts.

TRUE OBEDIENCE FLOWS FROM A HEART OF FAITH

So how do you motivate a man to do the things God wants him to do? Not by just telling him to do them, but rather by helping him to *want* to do what God wants him to do.

Manipulation and legalistic rule-making can make a man conform on the outside for a while—even decades. But the secret to lasting obedience is a renewed heart. Our goal is to help men believe the right things so they will live the right way.

There is really only one reason men don't build their life around their faith—they don't believe they can truly trust Christ. The Bible calls this unbelief. And since everything we do reflects what is in our hearts, all sinful attitudes and actions are a result of unbelief.

When a man works seventy hours a week just so he can get more power and money, he does so because he believes that is how he will find something that he cannot get any other way. When a man gets emotionally involved with a woman who is not his wife, he believes he will gain something that his wife, or God, cannot provide.

On the other hand, when men resist temptation and live righteously, they are often motivated by faith. "By faith [Moses] left Egypt, not fearing the king's anger" (Hebrews 11:27). Moses obeyed God rather than man not just because he decided he would or because someone else told him to but because he believed God.

When you work with a man, consider these questions: "How can I help his faith in God to grow?" "How can I help him understand even more fully that his hope is only in God?" "How can I help him develop a deeper love for Jesus Christ?" A heart filled with faith, hope, and love leads to a righteous, obedient life.

The Fruit and the Root

During a vacation a few years ago, David got angry with a member of his extended family. On the surface, the issue seemed to be a disagreement over a decision regarding the kids. After David thought and prayed about what was going on in his heart, he realized his anger came because someone implied he had made a mistake.

Like many men, one of the idols David often loves more than Christ is the idea of his own competence—that he is capable of accomplishing anything he attempts. So when his family member disagreed with his decision, it felt like he was accusing David of being wrong regarding the children. Since David couldn't accept that he was wrong without crushing his idol, he reacted with anger to protect his illusion of competence.

Men are often encouraged to deal with anger by taking a deep breath, counting to ten, and many other techniques. But this only deals with the surface. The deeper question is, "How can we help men deal with the anger in their hearts?"

Another example: Too much of the advice that has been available for men struggling with pornography has been purely behavioral. Get an Internet filter, find an accountability partner, drive home a different way so you don't pass the adult video store—all good things to do, and necessary if you struggle with this issue. But just as important is that we ask a man, "Why do you love looking at pictures of naked women more than you love Jesus? What do you think you're going to get from looking at pornography that you can't get from Christ?"

As men, we are tempted to try to fix things in our own strength by focusing on externals. So we get into an accountability group, use a budgeting system, avoid places of temptation, and add items to our calendars and to-do lists. None of these is bad, but each needs to be secondary. Often the externals deal with the fruit and not the root.

When we're confronting the issues men struggle with—anger, sexual addition, materialism, workaholism, emotional disconnection from their wife—God calls us to move past behavior to the heart issues involved.

Picking Off Oranges, Taping on Apples

We have lots of orange trees in central Florida where we live. If a person decided they didn't want an orange tree anymore, they could go out and pick off every orange. Next they could go to the store, buy a bagful of apples, then come home and duct tape apples all over the tree.

But what would happen? In a few weeks, the apples would rot. And next year? The oranges would be back. The only way to get rid of the oranges for good is to dig the tree up by the roots.

Often our system teaches men to "pick oranges and tape on apples." They deal with the symptoms of sin they can see, but they don't get to the root of how their sin flows out of unbelief. So even if they are able to use willpower to control their sin for a while, eventually it comes back stronger than ever. And in the meantime, their hearts are growing cold.

Christ offers men the chance to change from the roots, from the inside out. He calls us to stop making our strength our god, and start walking with Him by faith. Consider Jeremiah's words:

> Cursed is the one who trusts in man, who depends on flesh for his strength and whose heart turns away from the LORD. He will be like a bush in the wastelands; he will not see prosperity when it comes. He will dwell in the parched places of the desert, in a salt land where no one lives. But blessed is the man who trusts in the LORD, whose confidence is in him. He will be like a tree planted by the water that sends out its roots by the stream. It does not fear when heat comes; its leaves are always green. It has no worries in a year of drought and never fails to bear fruit. *(Jeremiah 17:5–8)*

When you help men develop their roots, you'll find more and more men moving beyond being involved in your ministry for what they can get. You'll have men who want to help other men experience what God has done for them.

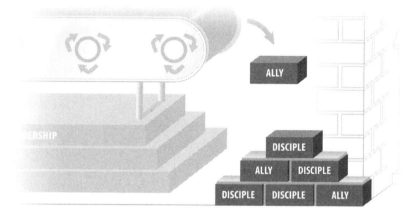

HELPING MEN BECOME ALLIES

Many men in your church probably look at your church's ministry as a set of mostly unrelated activities and tasks (see the portal priority chart in the next chapter). And you probably spend most of your time recruiting—begging—the men who are already sitting in your church to attend your events or activities. For the first event you make an announcement, the next time you add a testimony . . . and maybe the next time you have a few skydivers land on the church lawn as the service ends! So you spend all your time, money, creativity, and energy to get the men who are already at your church every week interested in your ministry to men. And you do it over and over again, event after event, year after year.

What's wrong with this picture? These are your committed men. Many of them should already feel a part of the vision and be excited about joining what God is doing.

How can you make a change? Men do what they want to do, and they will want to do things they see as valuable, worthwhile, or bringing happiness. It's your job to present the vision in such a way that the Holy Spirit can call men to passionate commitment. (We're going to help you do just that in chapter 8.)

Often we recruit men to tasks or events: "Can you bring the donuts to our next breakfast?" "Will you call the men and invite them to the retreat?"

"Will you please come to our luncheon?" There is one major problem—when you recruit men to tasks, you have to "sell them again" every time there is a new task that needs to be done or a new event to attend.

Instead, communicate about everything you do in terms of the vision of your ministry. (Chapter 8 will present a detailed discussion to help you define and communicate your vision.) If you ask a man to pick up bags of ice for the barbeque, say, "Tom, we're trying to reach every man in our community for Christ and help him join our band of brothers. That's why we're having this barbeque. Would you consider bringing the ice to help us reach these men and become a band of brothers?" It only takes thirty more seconds to cast the vision, and you still get your ice.

The vision will go in one ear and out the other for nineteen out of twenty men. But the payoff is with that one man. When a man buys into the vision and becomes an *ally*, you don't have to "sell" him on each separate activity or ministry. Each "task" becomes an opportunity for him to forward a cause he already believes in and be a disciple "sent to work for Christ."

An ally is a man who aligns himself with the vision God has given for the men of your church. He is willing to sacrifice and work to see that vision become a reality. He may or may not formally serve on the leadership team, but he is convinced that discipling men is a cause worth giving his life to. You don't have to beg an ally to be involved—he's grateful for opportunities to advance his ministry in the lives of other men.

There are three spheres of ministry to men in your church (see Figure 2). Many men's ministry leaders focus only on the total number of men involved in their ministry; for example, "Forty went on the retreat, twenty-seven came to breakfast, and nineteen are involved in small groups." These are great things to know, but you also need to focus on how many men are allies in the vision. Allies are not just attenders; they are advocates for your disciple-making efforts. Increase the number of allies every year and you will almost certainly have a vibrant and sustainable ministry to men. If this inner circle stops growing, watch out!

This is why it is so important for a leadership team not to be filled with workers but rather to be praying, strategizing, recruiting, and sharing the vision with other men. Leaders burn out, their life situation changes, and they move. The way you can keep sustaining the ministry is by continu-

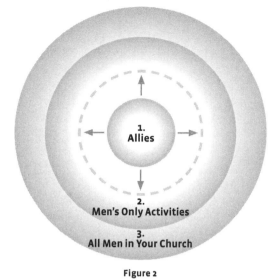

Figure 2
THREE SPHERES OF MINISTRY TO MEN IN YOUR CHURCH
1. The number of men who are allies with your vision and what God is doing
2. The men involved in your men's only activities—retreats, small groups, ministry projects, etc.
3. All the men who have any contact with your church

ously building more and more allies within your church.

As we've already said, men are looking to give their lives to something. Witness their commitment to golf, hunting, college football, their hobbies, and computer games. We need to lift up Christ's call in a compelling way. God will use our efforts to draw men to Himself.

Create an environment where the Holy Spirit can show men the attitudes and beliefs of their hearts. Don't allow men to go along to get along but call them into an authentic heart relationship with Christ. God will use your ministry not only to produce disciples but allies in the great adventure of seeing His kingdom become a reality in this world.

As God raises up allies for your ministry, be sure you know what you are actually going to do to disciple men. In the next chapter, we'll help you understand what it looks like to orient your church around the priority of discipleship.

Remember This

- Every day we choose whether to live by our own strength and be independent from God, or to depend on God alone and walk by faith.

- Men know how to play the game. If you let them, they will follow your rules to perfection. But in ten or twenty years they will realize their hearts are dead.

- With every decision, a man is choosing one thing over another. He makes his choices based on his worldview and his beliefs.

- Legalistic rule-making can only make a man conform on the outside for a while. The secret to lasting obedience is a renewed heart. Christ offers men the chance to change from the roots, from the inside out.

- Use methods that touch men's hearts—prayer, music, drama, film clips, testimonies, stories, and shared experiences.

- An ally is a man who aligns himself with the vision God has given for the men of your church. He is willing to sacrifice and work to see that vision become a reality.

- One key to sustainability is to make sure you are increasing the number of allies.

TALK ABOUT THIS

1. Why would a man seem okay on the outside, then one day walk away from his family or his faith? Most of us have known a man who did this. What were the circumstances?

2. Think back to a major change in your own life—quitting smoking, losing weight, etc. What caused you to make the decision to change? How would this relate to a man making the decision to allow God to change his heart?

3. Think back to a time when you had a moving experience with Christ through your church. What was that like? What lasting change did that bring in your life?

PRAY ABOUT THIS

Pray together as a leadership team . . .

• for any men in your church who may be like "Lou," that they would stop going through the motions and start pursuing an authentic relationship with Christ.

• that God would help you as leaders live out of an authentic and vibrant faith in Jesus Christ alone.

• that God would help you create an environment that He can use to touch men's hearts.

PART TWO

THE FOUNDATIONS
OF YOUR MINISTRY TO MEN

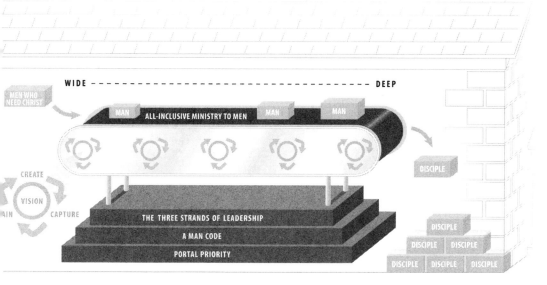

THE PORTAL PRIORITY
AND THE MAN CODE

To build a sustainable ministry to men, you'll need a solid foundation. Start with your focus. Yes, men need to be godly fathers, caring husbands, good stewards, and servant leaders. But what is the core issue? And how can we communicate it to men so they feel valued and inspired? Laying the right foundation can help disengaged men to connect with the ministry of your church.

THE BIBLE TELLS US, "Go and make disciples . . . baptizing them in the name of the Father and of the Son and of the Holy Spirit" (Matthew 28:19). Sometimes we get this confused with, "Go and make workers . . . browbeating them in the name of the Father and of the Son and of the Holy Spirit."

Jesus doesn't call churches to make "workers" but "disciples." The purpose of ministry, then, is to make disciples, not workers. Men don't enjoy being made to go on a forced march. True disciples become workers out of the overflow of their growing relationship with Jesus Christ.

The Bible does, however, call us to "pray" for workers: "The harvest is so great, and the workers are so few," [Jesus] told His disciples. "So pray to the one in charge of the harvesting, and ask him to recruit more workers for his harvest fields" (Matthew 9:37–38 TLB).

Too often we try to "make workers and pray for disciples." We set the agenda for our ministry and then pester men until they get involved. We make sure that we have all our slots for workers filled and then pray that somehow, someway, someone might become a disciple.

Here's a key idea: If your church and men's ministry focuses on getting men to do "works" rather than "making disciples," it will burn them out. You will lose all your steam.

Instead, focus on making disciples and then pray that God would raise up workers for His kingdom.

A PARABLE

Picture yourself as the president of a one-hundred person law firm. For years you have recruited lawyers but then left them on their own. Without guidance and training, they have done more harm than good. Unresolved cases have piled up, other law firms consider your firm an embarrassment, and the public thinks you are incompetent.

Suppose you go to your board of directors and ask to hire another twenty lawyers. They would say, "Are you nuts? You haven't trained the lawyers we have. Why would we let you hire more? We have a terrible reputation. In fact, several young people who interned with us have quit the law practice. You're fired!"

A law firm that doesn't produce capable lawyers is not much of a law firm at all. So what does this mean for a church that doesn't produce disciples?

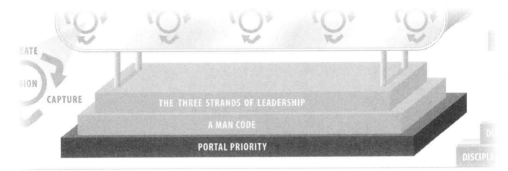

DISCIPLESHIP AS THE "PORTAL" PRIORITY

Jesus said, "Go and make disciples." That's interesting, because He could have said anything. He didn't say, "Go and make worshipers." He didn't say, "Go and make workers." Nor did He say, "Go and make tithers." Is Jesus interested in worshipers, workers, and tithers? Of course. But He knew we wouldn't get worshipers by making worshipers, and so forth. We get worshipers, workers, and tithers by making disciples.

Suppose a family has attended your church for three months. What will they think is the first priority—the organizing idea—of your church? One week they heard a sermon about the priority of worship. The next week they heard that they need to be cheerful givers. The following week they heard in Sunday school that committed believers go on mission trips. The week after that they were asked during the service to attend evangelism training. The next week in the small group they joined, they learned about compelling needs at the crisis pregnancy center. A weekend seminar greatly emphasized the importance of private study and devotions. If you were a new family, what would you think? It might look like an undifferentiated blob of disjointed activities:

Figure 3
Undifferentiated Church Priorities and Activities
(as they appear to a relative newcomer)

Looking at this collection of concepts, it is helpful to organize them into two sets: methods and outcomes. The middle items—godly families, service/missions, worship, fellowship, discipleship, evangelism, stewardship, social justice, and vocation—represent the outcomes most churches are trying to achieve. Your church may have a few more or less items in the list, but this is a good sampling of what most churches want their members to understand and live out in a biblical and godly way.

Yet, these are too many areas to focus on. There must be an organizing principle to help people understand, believe, and live out these objectives. That principle is discipleship.

Discipleship is the *portal priority* through which all the other priorities of a church can be achieved. Only by moving through the discipleship gateway can people truly affect their church and their church can affect them.

For instance, how can a man worship a God he doesn't know? Why would a man want to share his faith if he didn't understand the Great Commission? How could a man be a good steward if he didn't understand and believe that everything he has is a gift from God—his time, talent, and his treasures? As we disciple men's hearts, they start to live out of the overflow of their relationship with Christ. Therefore, we can organize these efforts by putting discipleship in the center and drawing arrows out to each of our other priorities like this:

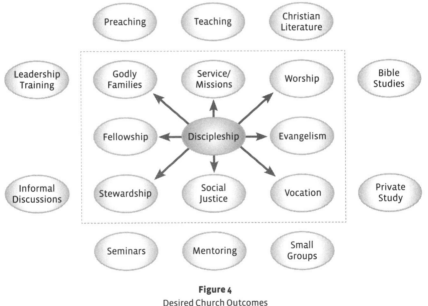

Figure 4
Desired Church Outcomes
Organized Around Discipleship as the Portal Priority

How can a church implement discipleship as the portal priority? The items around the outside of Figure 5 represent the activities, or methods, a church engages in to help build disciples.

Remember these activities are not ends in themselves but rather focus on helping people learn or live out what it means to be a disciple. Figure 5 illustrates this: All activities on the outside lead to discipleship in the middle. Now we have a clear picture of discipleship as the portal priority by

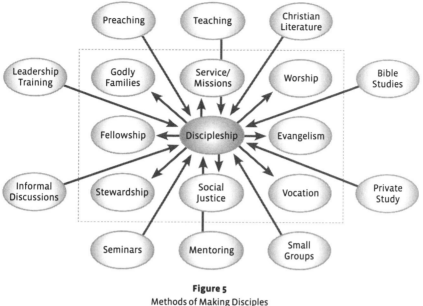

Figure 5
Methods of Making Disciples
to Reach Other Church Priorities and Goals

which every other goal of the church can be accomplished. For example, we don't preach to make worshipers but rather preach to help a man see God so that he can't help but worship.

To look at it a different way, rearrange *methods* and *outcomes* into two lists, with the methods of discipleship on the left, and the outcomes of discipleship on the right.

STEWARDS VERSUS DONORS

What steps might a church take to financially support its growing ministries? First, the pastor could preach about the responsibility of church members to tithe and support the work of the church. Next, teachers could teach about it in Sunday school classes and recommend books in the church bookstore; leaders could give all the small-group leaders announcements to read with some Scripture references here and there, even have a financial planning seminar for the church. But if you are preaching, teaching, reading, and announcing just to get the people attending the church to give money, you have a performance orientation. Your chart would look like Figure 6.

What's missing here is discipleship. You're not creating *stewards*; you're creating *donors*. So what does it mean to disciple men to be good stewards?

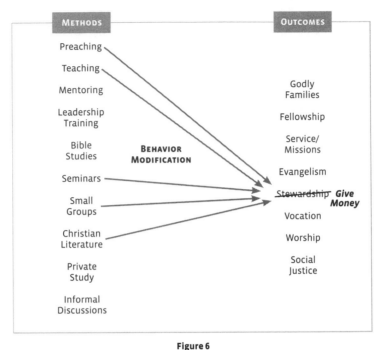

Figure 6
A Performance Orientation

First, we would preach, teach, and so forth not to guilt or obligate men to give so that we can meet the budget. In Mark 12:30–31, Jesus answers the question, "What is the most important commandment?" by saying, "'Love the Lord your God with all your heart and with all your soul and with all your mind and with all your strength.' The second is this: 'Love your neighbor as yourself.' There is no commandment greater than these."

In chapter 3, we described a disciple as "called, equipped, and sent." A man who has answered the call to give his life to Christ and is equipped as a disciple to know God will be motivated to love God and his neighbor. That man will respond to a need when it is presented to him, not out of guilt or obligation but out of the overflow of his relationship with Christ.

If you help a man love God with all his heart, mind, soul, and strength, and love his neighbor, then what kind of a response will you get from him when you teach him about stewardship? When you tell him about a need within the body? You won't have to tell him what to do or badger him; he will respond out of the *overflow* of his relationship with God, as shown in Figure 7.

Making discipleship the portal priority of our churches is the answer to what ails us. Consider our many systemic problems: divorce, fatherlessness, unwed mothers, drugs, alcoholism, abortion, crime, suicide, poverty, truancy, cheating, disrespect for authority. They all need attention. Beneath everything, though, is the need for a discipleship reformation of the Christian church. What single activity would have the greatest impact on all of these problems twenty years from now? Discipling men today.

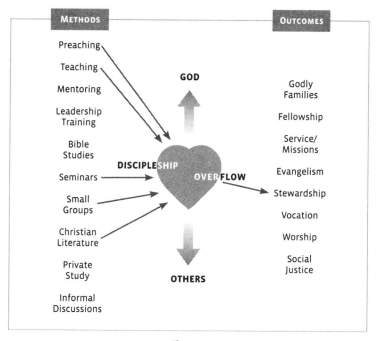

Figure 7
Serving God and Others
Out of an Overflowing Heart

A MAN CODE

When you make discipling men your portal priority, men will notice. As a matter of fact, they are already noticing a lot more about your church than you may think.

Quick . . . in a phrase or sentence, what's the dress code in your church? With just a second or two of thought, you probably came up with a description of what people wear: business casual; suit and tie; cowboy boots and blue jeans. One group from Hawaii said "shorts and thongs." (They meant sandals, of course.)

How do guys know this? Is there a sign out in front of your church: "First Community Church, Shirt and Tie Required"? Do you have fashion police standing at the doors letting only the appropriately dressed people in? Of course not. Men are smart. It doesn't take more than a week to figure out what to wear. Give us two or three weeks, and we'll be carrying the "correct" translation of the Bible; and in two months we'll be nodding and saying "Amen!" in all the right places during the sermon.

Just as your church has an unspoken—but well-known—dress code, it also has an unspoken "man code." The man code is the environment your church creates for men. Within a few weeks after beginning to attend, a man understands what it means to be a man in this church. Just like with the dress code, this impression isn't explicitly stated. Men soak it in from the atmosphere around them.

MESSAGES YOUR CHURCH SENDS TO MEN

What impression does your church give about the importance of men? How would you complete this statement: "Men Are _____ Here"?

"Important"? "Tolerated"? "Needed"? "Leaders"? "Supposed to do the hard work but leave the thinking to the women"? These are some of the answers we've received from church leaders who have attended courses at the Leadership Training Center at Man in the Mirror. One man said their man code was "If you'd like your wife and children to go to church, bring them here." Another said, "Successful men wanted here." Another's was, "If you think you're tired now, come to our church and we'll show you what tired really is!" Finally, one man said their man code was simply "Hi." Obviously, we've also had many positive man code statements as well.

THE BIG IDEA

Within a few weeks, a man understands what it means to be a man in your church.

What about your church? Imagine a new man comes to your church three or four times. In a phrase or sentence, how would he honestly sum up what he thinks it means to be a man in your church? Consider this question carefully and then write your man code in the space provided.

Since it's not something that is explicitly stated, how exactly do men figure out the "man code" of your church?

Entire books have been written on this subject, including *Why Men Hate Going to Church* by David Murrow (Thomas Nelson, 2005). He points out that every church has a "thermostat." Unfortunately, many churches' thermostats are set to "comfort." Men, Murrow says, need a thermostat set to "challenge." Stanley Allaby, a pastor for forty-two years in New England, is fond of quoting the adage, "My job is to comfort the afflicted, and afflict the comfortable." Men need to be "afflicted" out of their comfort zone.

Here are some other ways men learn to recognize the man code from the environment their church creates.

Impressions from the Leaders
Men look at the leaders. Men follow strong leaders. They like to know that their leaders are certain of where they are going and what they are saying. This isn't about browbeating or blind obedience, it's about confidence. If a

man doesn't believe in the leaders, he can't follow the vision.

This is particularly important to men who are either young or new to your church. When you hold up a leader as a standard for a mature Christian man, does he look boring, tired, and half dead? Or does he look vibrant, excited, and well-spoken (regardless of age)? Men should be able to look at the visible leaders in the church and say, "I want to be like that."

Impressions from the Music

Men listen to the music. While contemporary music may connect stylistically with the up-and-coming generations, some of those praise choruses aren't exactly "man friendly." Men resonate with songs that talk about the challenge, adventure, and battle of following Christ and seeing His kingdom become a reality. They tend to connect less with songs that ask Jesus to "hold me in Your arms."

Impressions from the Bulletin

Men read the bulletin. If your church bulletin has a section for women's ministry events, does it have a section with information for men? If not, what message does that send? More important than the amount of space the bulletin devotes to men, how does it communicate with the congregation in general? If your bulletin has articles in it, think about adding an article for men once in a while.

Be sure the bulletin makes strong statements about what God is doing through men in your church. "Men's Bible Study, Wednesday night, Room 202, 7:30 p.m." is not appealing to most men. How about " 'Disruptive Jesus: A Bible Study for Men.' Come learn how Jesus challenged the norm, and how it can have a radical impact on your life and our community. Wednesday night at 7:30 p.m. in Room 202"? Now, that's a Bible study that has a chance to catch men's attention.

Impressions from the Pastor

They listen to the pastor. Pastors, of course, have a tremendous impact on how men are viewed in the church. For instance, Pete Alwinson, pastor of Willow Creek Presbyterian Church (PCA) in Winter Springs, Florida (and Brett's pastor), makes a point of speaking directly to men in just about every sermon. Often he will say, "Men, this is what this means for us . . . " That sends a clear message that men matter in his church.

Impressions from the Setting

They look at the decor. Really . . . men notice the setting and pick up on its message.

We've noticed an interesting trend in church design: The ladies' bathroom is amazing. It's like a lounge: a couch, mirrors, counter space—a place where women can feel comfortable hanging out for a while. (Perhaps you're wondering how we know this.) Unfortunately, in many cases the ladies' room has begun to spill out into the rest of the church. Mauve window treatments, flowery wallpaper, pastel colors—all of these can send the message to men: "We've designed this space to make our women as comfortable as possible."

Get some guys on the decorating committee! Fight (nicely) to make the physical environment of your church man friendly. This is as simple as leather couches, striped wallpaper, earth tones—even some black-and-white nature photos on the wall instead of those pretty pictures of a mother holding her baby.

> ## Q & A
>
> ### Does "man friendly" mean anti-woman?
>
> Most women we've met would do whatever it took to get their husbands or sons into church. Women will buy into this concept of making the church "man friendly" when they're shown that it will get them what they want—the men in their lives growing in their faith.

Impressions from the Level of Quality

They look for quality. Men are extremely sensitive on this issue. While there certainly need to be times when the children's choir sings in thirteen-part disharmony, the church choir should not. Men don't think it's sweet when the drama troupe "tried really hard" but forgot their lines. Quality extends to the flyers you hand out to men, the events you hold for them, the materials you use in small groups and Sunday school, and even the Web site for the church.

Men today have become savvy consumers, and they are surrounded by sophisticated, high-quality marketing all the time. While you can't expect to compete with Madison Avenue, men can tell when there is a sincere effort to offer quality. If you think about it, the message we are delivering deserves our best efforts.

Impressions from the Use of Humor

They listen for humor. The men's ministry at David's church held an event for men called "Rise Up" where they were laying out the vision for men for the year. They invited men by calling it a *"Mandatory* Meeting for All University Presbyterian Church Men (unless you have a problem with authority, in which case, you're not allowed to come!)." When men see that everything doesn't have to be "prim and proper" (translation: boring), they get a sense that your church is a place where they can fit in.

At one Leadership Training Center class, a pastor from a Caribbean island responded to the banter between the Man in the Mirror faculty members—which is often playful and joking. He exclaimed, "I never realized that Christianity could be *fun!*"

A note of caution. Humor at the expense of men sends the wrong message. Don't make men—or an individual man—look stupid for a laugh, especially in mixed company. You would never tell racist or sexist jokes, so be careful about "stupid men" jokes.

Impressions from the Church's Vision

They listen for the vision. Men want to believe that God is doing something through your church. They want to be part of a church that is going somewhere. They want to know that being a man in your church matters. Reinforce the vision of your men as often as you can in ways that will resonate with them.

THE FOUNDATIONS FOR YOUR MINISTRY

You've started building a strong foundation for your men's ministry. A philosophy of ministry that says discipleship is your portal priority puts first things first, and encourages you to always focus on discipling men's hearts instead of correcting their behavior.

Making sure your man code makes men feel welcome increases the likelihood they'll hang around long enough for your ministry to make an impact in their lives.

In the next chapter we'll explain how leadership forms the final layer of your foundation.

REMEMBER THIS

- Jesus said, "Go and make disciples." He could have picked anything—workers, worshipers, tithers, for example. But He picked disciples.

- Discipleship is the portal through which we can achieve all the priorities of the church.

- When discipleship is not the portal priority, we often end up focusing on men's behavior rather than their hearts.

- When we disciple men to love God and their neighbors, they will live in a way that reflects this love.

- Every church has an unspoken—but well-known—man code, an impression it gives about what it means to be a man in this church.

- There are many cues that men pick up on to develop this impression: the leaders, music, bulletin, pastor, decor, quality, and vision. Well-placed humor helps too.

TALK ABOUT THIS

1. Do the nine outcomes shown in Figure 3 correspond with your church's priorities? What would you add or delete?

2. How does your church build disciples? Do you employ all of the methods on the outside of the box in Figure 3? What would you add or delete?

3. Pick an activity you are doing for men now. Does this activity focus on men's hearts or their behavior? How would you adjust it to focus more on discipleship?

4. Do you think your church has an environment that is male friendly? What does your church do that might make men—especially unchurched men—feel uncomfortable?

5. How could you improve your environment without making the women feel uncomfortable? Brainstorm your ideas using the list provided near the end of this chapter.

PRAY ABOUT THIS

Pray with your leadership team...

- that God helps you focus your ministry efforts to disciple men into a right relationship with Him.

- that your church's men—and your leadership team—would live out of the overflow of their relationship with Him.

- that God would help you provide a welcoming and engaging environment for men.

- that God will continue to help your leadership team grow closer as a band of brothers devoted to discipling men from the inside out.

THE THREE STRANDS
OF LEADERSHIP

Bill Bright, founder of Campus Crusade for Christ, was fond of saying, "Everything boils down to leadership." We believe him. Our experiences with churches that are discipling men bears this out. Your ministry with men will be a reflection of the leaders God raises up within your church. This chapter will help you gather and train leaders to sustain a vibrant ministry with men in your church.

IF YOU VISIT Amazon.com and enter "leadership" in the search box, you'll find over 18,500 books available. Why are there so many titles? Perhaps because everyone recognizes the importance of leaders. Or maybe it's because nobody seems to be able to get it right, so they keep buying more books about it.

This book may not be listed under "leadership" in the bookstore, but make no mistake: Leadership is the foundation of an effective disciple-making ministry. Nothing else you do will make any long-term difference without effective leadership. Without committed, involved leaders, it all falls apart. Leadership envisions, focuses, organizes, communicates, encourages, equips, perseveres, and celebrates. A ministry built on any other foundation simply will not work.

FOUNDATIONS FOR MEN'S MINISTRY
THAT DON'T WORK

Some leaders have tried to build their men's ministry on *emotion*. Reading the statistics we presented at the beginning of this book can energize a leader to want to make a difference! But emotion is not faith. Emotion will only carry you through a disappointment or two, and in men's ministry it doesn't take long to experience a lot of disappointment. Plus, guys can be put off by passion when it's not expressed in a healthy way. It can come off as, well, a little weird. No one wants to follow weird.

Some churches try to build their ministry on *obligation*. They find a few well-spoken guys who show up for everything and then convince them that the men's ministry is very important. A little guilt works well here. Just remind potential leaders that God calls us all to serve the kingdom and you know just the place for them. Your plan for the men in your church and community is simple: They just need to understand what the Bible says and then do it! Attend church faithfully, come to your men's events, help out on the workdays, and raise well-behaved children.

As crazy as this sounds, many men's ministries are built on the foundation of one slightly overzealous man who wants to tell everyone else what to do. If that's you, please stop!

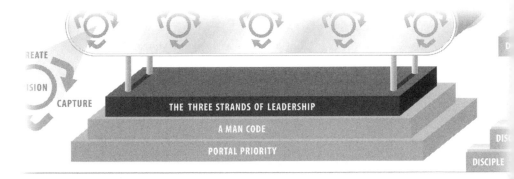

A WORD OF CAUTION

How long does it take for leaders to implement a successful men's ministry program? It takes a long time. Even Google, arguably one of the speediest success stories in corporate history, took over four years just to go live online. There really are no shortcuts. A "shortcut" takes years to develop.

Scholarly research indicates that, as a rule of thumb, about two-thirds of all program implementations fail. How does it happen? Here are a few reasons:

- Leaders think they can wing it.
- They don't put in the time required.
- They underestimate how long it takes to make a disciple.

- They underestimate how long it takes to get a program going.
- They underestimate the resistance to change they encounter.
- They are not equipped.
- They don't get training because they think, "This should be pretty easy. How hard could it be?"

Every time a men's ministry fails, it's like a little inoculation. Just like a flu shot keeps the flu virus from being able to live in your body, the church becomes more and more resistant to a sustainable men's ministry. The next leader who wants to build a men's ministry in the church encounters increased resistance. After three or four such failed attempts, the church's antibodies are fully developed and impenetrable. Men's ministry gets the reputation of "a loser." The pastor has decided, "That will never work here." Actually, it will, but a made-up mind is almost impossible to change.

Research seems to indicate that unless a leader devotes at least five—and more likely ten—years to an initiative, success is unlikely. So unless you are willing to devote ten or more years to building a men's program, it would be better for the Christian men's movement if you didn't start. These are serious times that require serious leaders willing to devote serious effort for a serious length of time.

If you are in the game for the long haul, here's the kind of leadership structure you should consider.

THE THREE STRANDS OF LEADERSHIP

Solomon wrote, "A cord of three strands is not quickly broken" (Ecclesiastes 4:12). Your men's ministry will need three strands of leadership to reach its highest potential: (1) the senior pastor, (2) a primary leader for your men's discipleship efforts, and (3) a team of leaders to support him. You need the proper buy-in at each of these levels to have a well-balanced foundation.

You may be thinking, "But it's just me and the pastor carrying the ball on this right now. I don't have a leadership team." Or, "We've got a great team and a passionate leader, but our pastor doesn't pay much attention to discipling

> ## THE **BIG** IDEA
>
> The three strands of leadership for your ministry are the senior pastor, a primary leader, and a leadership team.

NO MAN LEFT BEHIND

men." Or, "Our pastor is behind us, but no one guy has really stepped up. We work by consensus."

Building your men's ministry without these three strands of leadership is like driving a car with a missing spark plug. The car will still run, but not like it should. It will sputter and misfire, lacking the power of an engine hitting on all cylinders.

LEADER STRAND #1:
THE SENIOR PASTOR'S ENTHUSIASTIC INVOLVEMENT

Tom is a lay leader in his church. An accomplished businessman, Tom was adept at organizing and influencing. Luckily for his church, Tom also had a heart for small groups.

For years Tom labored, with the blessing and public support of his pastor, building up a small-group ministry in his church. He prayed, recruited group leaders, oversaw training, organized curriculum, counseled, and worked his heart out. After seven years, he was able to build a small-group ministry in his church with over one hundred adults each week.

When a Pastor "Catches the Bug"

Then, his pastor caught the small-group "bug." Suddenly, he realized how effective small groups could be for the spiritual development of his congregation.

So one spring, with the counsel and support of his elders and Tom himself, the pastor began a series of sermons about community and small groups. Over the course of several months, he laid out before the congregation the importance of relationships. He decided to cancel their normal Wednesday night activities and replace it with a designated "home group night."

That fall, on the first Wednesday of the new initiative, over seven hundred adults participated in small groups.

Tom worked for seven years to build a small-group ministry with one hundred people. Then the senior pastor sets a date, preaches a few sermons, reorganizes the schedule, and—voila!—seven hundred people get involved. Clearly, a pastor's involvement is important.

Your pastor will ultimately determine where the primary intellectual, financial, and spiritual resources of the church are invested. If the senior pastor is involved in a program or initiative, it will get a budget, staff support, rooms when they need it, and plenty of publicity.

Support is not involvement. Our research suggests that support of the ministry by a pastor is good, but involvement is a lot better. If your pastor takes a personal interest in the process and health of your discipleship ministry with men, you have a huge head start.

This issue is one of the major complaints we hear from men's ministry leaders. "My pastor is just not behind us." "Our pastor never attends our men's events." "The men's activities barely get a mention from the pulpit."

That's ironic, because every pastor wants to see his men become disciples. But many pastors have been burned by men's ministry. In the past they have supported it, defended it, invested their time, and given it creative energy. But men's ministry didn't want to work. This was repeated for two, three, and maybe even four failed attempts.

So if you were the pastor, and for the fourth time in eight years, some enthusiastic (or perhaps naive) guy excitedly said to you, "Pastor! I've got this great idea! We should start a men's ministry!" what would you do? You'd smile, and nod, and wish him well. Then you'd just wait.

This is not cynicism, just reality. Pastors are responsible to a multitude of constituencies—all of them wanting the pastor to make their ministry his top priority.

Bringing the Pastor Aboard

So if your pastor does not jump on board at the beginning, that's okay. Be patient and persevere. There are also some ways you can help your pastor get involved in the men's ministry faster.

- *Pray for and with your pastor.* Here's one idea: Gather your men on Sunday mornings before services start and have a time of prayer for your pastor. Ask for specific requests. And don't just do it with the ulterior motive of getting him on board.
- *Support your pastor.* The men's ministry leadership team needs to have a reputation of enthusiastic support for your pastor. For example, discover his area of passion in ministry and rally around him to make him even more effective.
- *Inform your pastor.* Never let your pastor be surprised by what's going on in your ministry to men in the church. For example, copy him

on your summary e-mails after meetings and forward him stories of changed lives.

- *Include your pastor.* Invite your male pastor to your events, but include him in the way he wants to be included. He may not want to say the blessing or close in prayer; let him be one of the guys.
- *Love your pastor.* Find tangible ways for the men's leaders to show your pastor their appreciation. For example, set up a co-op to take care of his lawn for six weeks during the summer to free him up for vacations and refreshment.

A pastor who is prayed for, supported, informed, included, and loved tangibly by his men will be much more likely to be involved in their efforts to grow closer to Christ. In fact, that pastor will want to participate in making that happen, throwing the full resources of the church behind the effort. It will be good for your men, and good for your pastor. (Turn to appendix A for twenty-five more ideas for connecting with your pastor.)

LEADER STRAND #2: A PASSIONATE LEADER

An effective ministry to men needs a leader with an arrow through his heart for the men in your church and community. Someone needs to wake up in the morning thinking, "How can I help the men in our church to grow in their faith?"

Does he have to be a paid staff member? No. Could he be? Certainly. It would be great if your church paid a minister to devote a major portion of his time to men's ministry. If it's the senior pastor, even better. But for most churches, the men's ministry leader will be a layman.

What other qualifications are there for the men's ministry leader? In a few minutes you could come up with a healthy list, but from our work these are the three most important attributes:

First, he should be a man who loves God. Your men's ministry leader should be modeling what he hopes other men to become: a disciple (follower) of Jesus Christ. He should be growing spiritually, spending regular time in the Word, and able to talk comfortably about his faith with other men.

He doesn't need to be a Bible scholar or a great preacher or teacher. That's the pastor's job. While your men's ministry leader needs to be in the Scriptures regularly, he doesn't have to be able to translate from the original Greek.

Second, he should have a heart for men. Leaders in your church have different passions and callings. The men's ministry leader must have a passion for reaching and discipling men. And this needs to be his primary area of ministry in the church.

Third, he should have the right set of gifts to lead other leaders. How can you tell? Look for a man who has the respect of other men. This does not necessarily mean he needs to be well known or popular. But frankly, there are too many men's leaders out there who "self-selected" themselves. They have the passion but not the gifts. Be careful not to promote someone past the level of their competency as a reward for faithful service. Don't stop a man from ministering effectively where he is so that he can lead ineffectively in a new position.

LEADER STRAND #3: A COMMITTED LEADERSHIP TEAM

Surrounding the leader should be committed men who share many of the attributes of the leader himself. The height of your men's ministry will be determined by the depth of your leadership.

Q & A

Reflecting the Men You Want to Reach

Your men's ministry will become whatever your leadership team becomes. In other words, your leadership team should *look* like the guys you are trying to reach. If you want to reach men of all ages, your leadership team needs to have leaders from several different generations. If you want to reach men of different ethnic backgrounds, your leadership team needs to be ethnically diverse.

Everyone on your leadership team does not have to have the same level of spiritual responsibility or authority. Some members can play more of a implementation role while you are mentoring them for leadership. So, if you want to reach men at various levels of spiritual maturity, you

Here's a radical question: Should we have non-Christians on our leadership team?

You may think this is a silly question. Of course, you're not going to ask this guy to take on a spiritual leadership role, but is there a better place for a guy who is seeking Christ than to be around Christian men who have a passion for discipleship? An earnest seeker who has been around for a while may help your leadership team understand the perspective of the men you are trying to reach.

might want to invite some guys at various places on their spiritual journey.

Encourage each leader to live his life in such a way that others can tell he has been "with Jesus" (see Acts 4:13). As a team, encourage the men to become to each other what they want their church to become. That will create a model so attractive that other men will want to be part of it. As Tom Skinner, the late evangelist, often said, "We must become the live demonstration here on earth of what is happening in heaven, so that any time anyone wants to know what is happening in heaven all they have to do is check with us."

Involving Others and Staying Fresh

Finally, don't turn your leadership team into an "operations" or event committee. Your leadership team should be a prayer and strategic planning team, not a "doing" team. If you are planning a men's BBQ, then the leader who is responsible for the food should not decide on the menu, make a shopping list, buy the groceries, cook the food, and do the dishes. Rather, this is an opportunity to recruit men to these various tasks so they can begin to catch the vision. Bringing sodas is building the kingdom, but most men won't know that unless a leader shows them how their contribution reaches men with the gospel. (Again, that's casting the vision.)

We can't reiterate this point too strongly. If your leadership team is doing all the work, you can either disband now or wait a few years for it to fall apart. You may want to go ahead and make a tee time for Saturday because your ministry with men will not last unless you are constantly expanding the circle of men who believe in the vision.

> Recruiting is hard work. It is often easier to just do it yourself. DON'T. DON'T. DON'T. If you want your ministry to last, constantly give away the work of the ministry to men who may become your future leaders.

One question we often hear is, "How big should my leadership team be?" You might be tempted to decide by thinking through potential areas of responsibility: A small-groups coordinator, a big-events coordinator, a retreat coordinator, and so on. Sounds pretty well coordinated, doesn't it? But this approach is dangerous.

Men's leaders often tell us they are exhausted. It doesn't take long to discover they are trying to do small groups and a retreat and a softball team and a bus to Promise Keepers and an outreach event and on and on. Why? Because they think that's what men's ministries are "supposed" to do.

This brings about two problems: First, they're burning themselves out.

Second, nobody else wants to join the leadership team because they see how much work it is.

> "The size of our ministry determines the size of our leadership team" is hazardous. Instead, look at it this way: "The size of our leadership team determines the size of our ministry." God has placed certain men in your church with the desire to reach and disciple men. But for most of them it's not some vague calling; it's specific. Some feel passionate about softball, some about getting guys to go to Promise Keepers, some are into small groups, etc. Your ministry should flow out of the passions of your leadership team. If you don't have a guy who's passionate about retreats, then don't have a retreat. Believe it or not, "Thou shalt take thy men into the wilderness to retreat" is not actually in the Bible.

The men God has given you are not assets to accomplish the tasks set forth in your strategic plan. They are leaders. Their passions are wonderful clues to what God would have you do for the men of your church. If you allow them to pursue their calling, they will be more engaged, your ministry will be more effective, and, best of all, more leaders will be attracted. Your ministry will grow naturally, and in God's own time.

THE ARTT OF RECRUITING LEADERS

Recruiting leaders is a process. Here's a nice way to remember how this plays out in relationships: Appointment-Relationship-Trust-Task, or ARTT. How does this work?

Appointment

Create value for leaders by getting the *appointment*. The first time we saw our future wives, most of us didn't walk up and say, "Would you like to get married?" Instead, we asked for the appointment: a date for Friday night. So don't set your sights on a man and ask him to join your leadership team. Instead, ask for the appointment.

"Hey, John. I'd really like to get your feedback about our men's ministry. How would you like to get together for coffee one morning?" The value for John is that you are asking him for feedback. If he really is a potential leader, he'll be happy to meet with you.

Relationship

During your appointment, start building a *relationship*. Tell him about your involvement and why it is important to you. Listen to his heart. *But don't ask him to make a commitment to anything!* Be satisfied with becoming his friend.

Trust

After you share your passion for men's ministry, be ready with a right next step. If he is indifferent, ask him how you can pray for him. If he is too busy to be more involved, offer to pray for him and ask him to pray for you and the men. If he is interested in going further, ask him to come to your next leadership team meeting as a guest. He can sit in and hear what's going on. Then you can meet again and talk about it.

By offering a next step that is appropriate to his level of interest and availability, you show him that you are interested in helping him fulfill God's mission for his life, not your mission for his life. *Trust* begins to develop.

Task

Trust is the key to actually doing something together. Once he shows an ongoing interest, then you can offer him a *task*—either through asking him to pray or to explore getting involved. Don't rush this process or you will scare away your potential leaders.

DOUBLE THE SIZE OF YOUR LEADERSHIP TEAM...

If there is one common complaint about leaders, it's this: There are not enough of them. So here's an easy way to double the size of your leadership team.

Let's say you have four committed men on your leadership team. Make a covenant with each other to take one man to coffee or lunch each month and share why discipling men is important to you. Use your "elevator speech" (see chapter 8). Follow this process for a year. Assuming each of you misses a month here or there, you will have conversations with at least forty men.

Your passion will not mean much to many of these men. Others will be glad for you, but too busy to get involved themselves. But if just two out of every ten men express an interest in sitting in on a meeting (that means eight of your forty men), and half of those decide to get involved, you will have doubled the size of your leadership team in just a year!

. . . Or Cut Your Leadership Team in Half

It is hard work to build your leadership team. It is very easy to tear it apart. If your ministry is effectively discipling men, your leadership team will be attacked by the Enemy. That's why it's so important that each member of your leadership team be accountable to other godly men. Every man needs someone who can look him in the eye and tell when something doesn't seem right.

Also, living in a fallen world means that leaders may be taken out of the game by events beyond their control. Family illness, a job transfer, or other circumstances may prevent a man from continuing on your leadership team.

But the quickest way to cut your leadership team in half is this: Try to sculpt a man into a better leader. It's a mistake to try chiseling away the ungodly parts of a man so that only the good stuff is left. It very rarely works that way.

Our friend Dennis Puleo has been a successful entrepreneur and consultant for over twenty years. Dennis is also an outstanding motivator, and works with leaders through Man in the Mirror. In the Leadership Training Center, he often says, "Leaders need to be cultivated." Cultivation is an agricultural term. You cultivate a crop by choosing good seeds, preparing the soil, fertilizing it, and watering it regularly. Then you reap the harvest.

Leaders need to be polished, not chiseled. You polish leaders by encouraging them, not criticizing. By affirming them, not correcting. Make sure your leaders have plenty of opportunities to be exposed to the love of Christ. If you want a better leader, help him become a better disciple.

There have been many times, according to Dennis, when he has been asked by business acquaintances to come in and "light a fire" under their people. "They've got it all wrong," he says. "The idea is to find people already on fire and just pour some gasoline on them."

The High Calling of Leadership

It is a high calling to be a part of a team of men who desire to disciple men. Our prayer is that God will use your team to raise up scores, hundreds, or even thousands of men who would be valiant warriors for Christ's kingdom.

To summarize, the three foundations of a sustainable disciple-making ministry to men in your church are:

- a philosophy of ministry that says discipleship is the portal priority;
- an environment that communicates the proper man code to men; and
- a leadership strategy focused on three strands—your pastor, a leader, and your leadership team.

As you establish the foundation for your ministry, the next step will be to define the process you want to engage men in. The wide-deep continuum illustrates the path to become a mature disciple. We'll show you how this works in detail in the next chapter, and show you what activities in the church can help men along on this journey.

REMEMBER THIS

- Every time a men's ministry fails, it's like a little inoculation—your church builds up a resistance to men's ministry that is harder to overcome.

- "A cord of three strands is not easily broken." The three strands of leadership necessary for your men's ministry are: the enthusiastic involvement of the senior pastor, a passionate leader, and a committed leadership team.

- The pastor's tacit support won't mean a lot; his active support is okay; his enthusiastic involvement is best.

- The men's ministry leader should have a heart for God, a heart for men, and the leadership gifts necessary to lead other leaders.

- The height of your men's ministry will be determined by the depth of your leadership.

- The men of your leadership team should become to each other what they want the men of the church to become.

- Leaders need to be polished, not chiseled. They don't need you to light a fire under them—they're already on fire. Just find a way to pour some gasoline on them, then get out of their way!

TALK ABOUT THIS

1. What is the history of men's ministry in your church? When you say "men's ministry," what impression does it give people who are not involved? How can good leadership help you overcome or build on this impression?

2. Does your pastor believe that the men of your church—or at least the men's leaders—support and love him? What would you be willing to do to show him you are behind him 110 percent?

3. Are you feeling a little burned out on men's ministry? Have you started to notice your fellow leaders feeling the same way, or have you even already lost some? Why do you think this is? What can you do about it?

4. Take a few moments and list the names of the men currently involved on your leadership team. List the one or two things each of you is passionate about. Prayerfully consider whether these are the things God wants your men's ministry to focus on right now.

5. In chapter 12 you will develop a plan to recruit new leaders. Spend a few minutes brainstorming, and start a list of men with whom you might want to connect.

PRAY ABOUT THIS

Pray together as a leadership team . . .

• that your pastor will not just support your ministry but personally become involved.

• that God will bless your pastor's efforts to reach men.

• that God will raise up a man—if He hasn't already—who is passionately committed to giving every man in your church an opportunity to become a disciple of Jesus Christ.

• that God will help each member of your leadership team discern the role He has called them to in that effort.

An All-Inclusive
Ministry to Men

If you have one hundred men in your church, how big is your ministry? Sometimes our assumptions and paradigms limit us from seeing the bigger picture. This is certainly true of ministry with men. This chapter will drop-kick a few our common paradigms—and help you understand how your church can maximize the kingdom impact of every interaction you have with every man.

A CHURCH WE HAVE worked with was having its annual men's retreat. A few of the men from the leadership team became a subcommittee and took on the task of organizing it. They set some goals:

- Reach out to men who didn't traditionally attend their church's events.
- Help men get to know each other on the retreat.
- Develop a follow-up strategy that kept men involved after the retreat.

They worked hard to promote the event, and eighty guys registered, including twelve who were not very involved in the church and had never been on a retreat before. They had a businessman speak on a very practical level about how being a Christian affects your everyday life. The talks were short and had plenty of discussion time afterward. In order to make the new men feel comfortable, they allowed the men to sit wherever they wanted during the sessions and discussions.

They had lots of fun and competitive activities. And they offered a follow-up activity for guys to get involved in—smaller groups of men who would meet for six weeks to go deeper into the issues raised by the event.

During the retreat, it seemed as though guys were really getting to know each other. The discussion times were robust. The activities were fun and a lot of laughing and joking occurred throughout the weekend. At the end of the retreat, sixty men signed up for the follow-up, including eight of the twelve "fringe" men.

A Successful Retreat . . . or Not?

A week or two later, the entire men's ministry leadership team met, including the retreat planning team. The men's ministry team leader opened the meeting with a time to debrief the retreat. The retreat team was excited to talk about their success and frankly eager for a few pats on the back. What they heard next blew them away.

"Well," said one of the leaders, shifting uncomfortably, "I guess I'll start. I have to say I was really disappointed in the retreat this year. I just feel like we wasted an opportunity."

"Yeah, me too," added another leader. "For instance, the speaker hardly talked about really spiritual things at all. He didn't teach from the Bible; he mostly spoke about his own experiences."

"And the discussion times . . . " another man began. "Every time we were with different guys. We should have assigned guys to groups of four and stuck with those guys for the whole weekend. We could have met and prayed together, and hopefully gotten into some deep issues."

There were other comments about the speaker, Scripture memorization, guided private devotionals, and other "missed opportunities" from the retreat. The planning team was stunned. They had met every goal they had set for the weekend, yet the leadership team was ripping it apart. What went wrong?

WIDE – DEEP

The Wide-Deep Continuum

Making disciples is all about taking men who don't know Christ and helping them become mature, passionate followers of Jesus. This journey can be represented by a continuum:

MEN WHO NEED CHRIST - MATURE DISCIPLES

Your ministry to men will need to help men at every stage of this journey. We call this concept the *wide-deep continuum.*

WIDE - DEEP

Every man in your church can be placed somewhere on the continuum, and that determines the offerings that will appeal to him. As a man matures in his faith, he will move farther down the continuum.

How could knowledge of this continuum have helped the leadership team from the retreat example above? First of all, the planning team could have shared their goals with the rest of the leadership team and received their support and "buy-in" to the approach. All disappointment is the result of unmet expectations. The leadership team had one set of expectations about the target audience for the retreat; the planning team had another.

Notice that none of the suggestions that the other members of the leadership team made was bad. Teaching straight through passages of Scripture, staying with the same group of men for deeper discussions, having longer personal times with God—these are all great retreat activities to deepen men's faith.

But there was also nothing wrong with the type of retreat the team actually planned. It all depends on where you are aiming on the continuum.

APPLYING THE WIDE-DEEP CONTINUUM

You will interact with men at all points along this wide-deep continuum. On the left, or "wide," side are men who are not all that interested in spiritual things. To reach guys on the wide side, you need activities that reach them at their point of interest. These are activities that require little or no preparation and low commitment. Typical activities at the wide end are softball teams, BBQs, a Super Bowl party, golf, hunting, or fishing.

To reach men on the "deep" side, you need activities that meet their spiritual needs more deliberately. These activities probably have a connection from week to week; they require preparation; they'll go deeper into biblical concepts; they will offer accountability and transparency; and their focus will be on more mature Christians. Typical activities might include small groups, Bible studies, leadership training, service projects, or spiritual retreats.

> ## THE BIG IDEA
>
> Build a seamless process to move men across the wide-deep continuum.

No activity you plan can meet the needs of every man in your church. In our illustration of the retreat above, the retreat planning team was focused on reaching guys more to the left of this continuum, while the rest of the leadership team were hoping for something reaching guys on the right of the continuum.

As you plan, make sure you are offering different types of activities to reach the different types of men in your church. Build a seamless process to move men across the wide-deep continuum.

Also, be sure your leaders are clear about your target audience. Left to their own devices, your leaders will naturally tailor events to their passion and calling. Help them understand the purpose of the event so they can support the agreed upon agenda of the team.

LEADERSHIP TEAMS AND THE CONTINUUM

Different leaders will be passionate about reaching different types of men. As an example, consider this hypothetical situation at your church one Sunday morning:

Your men's ministry leadership team has just finished a prayer time before the service. An usher approaches and tells your team that two men are in the lobby asking for someone to talk to them.

One man has wandered in off the street. He is not sure why he is there, but he seems a little down and said that he is looking for answers. He wants to know what this Christianity thing is all about. The second man has been involved in the church for a while. Due to personal circumstances in his work and marriage, he really wants to take his relationship with Christ to the next step. He wants someone to talk with him about how to study the Bible and pray.

Quick! You have to choose only one. Which man would you rather go talk with?

Some of you reading this book have a heart for evangelism. Your desire is to reach out to lost souls and point them toward the cross. Others are more drawn toward helping Christian men build the kingdom of God. You like to help men understand what it means to study God's Word and pray. When we present this scenario to men at our Leadership Training Center (LTC), about half of the leaders want to talk to the man who is seeking Christ for the first time, while the other half feel drawn to talk to the man who is seeking a deeper relationship with Christ.

Think back to the continuum. Men at the left side of the continuum are seekers, trying to find their way to Christ. Men on the right side are leaders, wanting to follow Christ more closely and serve Him. *Most leaders are wired to work with men at a certain point on the continuum.* When you grasp this concept, it can help save a lot of trouble and misunderstanding.

After sharing this during one LTC course, a pastor and the men's ministry leader from his church came up and said, "You may have just saved our relationship."

The pastor explained that he would go out into the community and meet new men and convince them to give the church a try. But every time a new man walked in, his men's ministry leader would talk to them, invite them to join a small group, and explain the importance of accountability.

"As fast as I could get new guys in the front door," the pastor said, "they were running out the back." Understanding the continuum helped them realize that their hearts were for men at different places.

The layman learned that every man has to go through a process. They're not always ready for accountability and transparency. He and the pastor agreed to develop an appropriate process to move men along the continuum.

WIDE -- -- -- -- -- -- -- -- -- -- -- -- -- -- -- -- DEEP

MAN ALL-INCLUSIVE MINISTRY TO MEN MAN MAN

THE WIDE-DEEP CONTINUUM AND YOUR CONVEYOR BELT

The conveyor belt in our image includes all the activities and interactions that your church has with men. It's these interactions and activities that engage men and help them move forward in their spiritual journey. But it's a fallacy to think that all of these interactions have to be men's only activities driven by the traditional idea of a men's ministry.

How Many Men Are in Your Men's Ministry?

Think about your church for a moment. In the spaces below, write down the answers to these two questions:

How many men do you have in your church? _____
How many men do you have in your men's ministry? _____

We ask this question at every training class we do in Orlando. While the answers may vary, we typically get answers like: 500 men, 50 in our men's ministry; 100 men, 20 in the men's ministry; 75 men, and we don't really even have a men's ministry.

Who are the men you think of as being "in" your men's ministry? Is it the guys who come to your monthly men's breakfast? The twelve guys who gather on Wednesday mornings at 6:00 a.m. for Bible study? The last group of men who went on the retreat?

We'd like you to consider looking at this concept differently: *Everything your church does that touches any man is men's ministry. Everything.* So if you have one hundred men in your church, then the size of your men's ministry is one hundred. The only question is, "Is it an effective or ineffective ministry?"

As we said earlier, "Your system is perfectly designed to produce the results you are getting." We also said that your church's ministry with men is perfectly designed to produce the men you have sitting—and not sitting—in your pews.

What would happen if you started thinking of your men's ministry in these terms?

- Every man in my church is part of the men's ministry.
- Everything our church does for and through a man is men's ministry.

An all-inclusive men's ministry tries to maximize the kingdom impact of every interaction with every man, no matter the setting. Singing on the praise team, parking cars, working with the youth, doing volunteer accounting, or sitting in the Sunday worship service—it is all ministry to and through men. The job of a leader is to determine how to help men be discipled in each of these contexts.

An All-Inclusive Mind-Set Solves Typical Problems

An all-inclusive view of your ministry to men helps eliminate the "us versus them" mentality that sometimes develops between men in the church. Any growing church has lots of men who are working hard every week in faithful ministry. Many of these men are simply unable to also be involved in your men's only activities. It's foolish to imply that a deacon who spent two and a half hours installing a new dishwasher for a single mom is not part of the men's ministry because he does not get up for the 6:30 a.m. Bible study the next morning. These are exactly the kind of men we are trying to produce, and they are a vital part of what God is doing through the men of our churches.

A church David worked with during a consulting weekend shared one of their "problems." Their church was reaching lots of young fathers in the community through their family sports program. This often led to them getting involved in marriage activities and children's events. Some of these men were going through a structured leadership training and beginning to serve in leadership positions in the church. The leaders said, "We have a problem. We have these young men in our church who were reached through our

> ## THE **BIG** IDEA
>
> An all-inclusive men's ministry maximizes the kingdom impact of every interaction with every man, no matter the setting.

sports programs. Now they are serving as deacons and elders and they have never come to any of our men's ministry events."

David restated it for them. "OK, let's see if I have this right. You have men in the community who did not have a relationship with Christ. Your church reached them through your children's sports ministry. These men and their wives became connected with other families and the church. They are growing as Christians. They are becoming leaders and actually serving as leaders in your church. And the problem is . . . ?"

Together they were able to see that this really wasn't a problem at all. The only problem was that as leaders they had a stunted view of what constituted ministry to men.

If everything the church does that touches men is men's ministry, then you have a vested interest in helping every ministry succeed. The other ministries in the church should believe that the men, and the men's ministry leadership, are eager for them to fulfill the mission God has given them.

An all-inclusive men's ministry will leverage the efforts of the other ministries in the church to help you achieve your purpose of discipling men. Rather than reinventing a men's only activity every time, throw your weight behind some events your church has already planned that reach men. It's not appropriate for us to say to men, "We'll disciple you if you come to our activities or events." Jesus didn't say, "Come and be discipled." He said, "Go and make disciples." God is calling us to go where our men are and disciple them there.

As part of a men's leadership team, you don't have to do all the heavy lifting. Your church is probably already doing things that are working to disciple men. Remember, every activity that reaches men is men's ministry. Take advantage of the classes, groups, and processes that are making male disciples in your church. Help the leaders and men in these settings see them as opportunities to disciple men.

Support other events and ministries in the church by adopting them as part of your ministry to men. For instance, as a men's ministry, do all the setup and breakdown of your next big outreach activity sponsored by the outreach team. Offer to recruit the male volunteers for your children's ministry summer day camp or Bible school. Rally your men around the next workday sponsored by your grounds committee.

NOT ANOTHER DEMAND ON YOUR PASTOR

An all-inclusive ministry mind-set leverages the work and contribution of your pastor. Think about it. If everything your church does that touches men is part of your men's ministry, then your pastor is the "tip of the spear," so to speak, of your efforts to disciple men. It will be a relief for your pastor to know that you don't have to invent a whole new set of programs to have a men's ministry. Help him understand that your intention is for all the things your church is already doing with men to become even more effective. Brainstorm with him how to make your church more male-friendly and how to support the leaders of other ministries. Getting your pastor to think about how to disciple men in your church may be the single greatest contributor to the success of your ministry.

UNEXPECTED LEADERS

Not just your pastor benefits from an all-inclusive men's ministry approach. Just as important, we need to inspire other leaders in the church to see every interaction they have with men as a disciple-making opportunity.

For example, just about every church has ushers. If you were to ask the head usher in your church, "What is the purpose of the ushers? Why are these men (and/or women) here?" he might say nice things like, "To serve people by making sure they know what's going on and helping them find a seat," or, "To help maintain the atmosphere of worship throughout the service as people come in and out." In the end, his answer probably will boil down to handing out bulletins and getting people to sit down—the quicker the better.

What if you could inspire your head usher to a new vision: Why are these men here? "To become disciples of Jesus Christ." What would happen if he was able to see his role as *primarily* to help disciple the other ushers, and *only secondarily* to get people seated? Here's an example that shows how you can do this:

Week One. The head usher tells all of the other ushers that he would like them to get there five minutes early next week. He has something he wants to share with them. He calls them all on Saturday to remind them.

Week Two. Five minutes earlier than usual, he gathers the ushers and hands them all two business cards—one is blank, the other has a Bible verse on it. He reads the verse to them and tells them why it is a meaningful verse:

" 'There are different kinds of gifts, but the same Spirit. There are different kinds of service, but the same Lord. There are different kinds of working, but the same God works all of them in all men' (1 Corinthians 12:4–6). Guys, this verse shows that everyone who serves is playing an important part. Pastor is serving God with his preaching, and we're serving the same God by helping people get bulletins and find seats. We're all an important part of a person's worship experience.

"Put this card in your wallet and pull it out this week when you have a minute. You may even want to memorize the verse.

"I'd like to pray for each of you, so on the blank card just write down your name and something you'd like me to pray about this week. Let me say a quick prayer now and I'll collect the cards in a minute or two.

" 'Dear Lord, thank You for the opportunity to serve You this morning. Thank You for these men and women who are willing to give up their time to be an usher. Help us remember You as we go through life this week. Bless our families and our church for Your glory. Amen.' "

Weeks Three and Four. He does the same thing. But he starts to ask them if they have any thoughts about the verse, and if there are any prayer requests they'd like to share with the group.

Week Five. This week the head usher only gives each person the card with the Bible verse. After he goes over it and they talk for a few minutes, he asks them to write their name and prayer request on the back of the card and trade with each other.

As time progresses, they meet a few minutes earlier to accommodate the discussions that have started happening. Different guys start praying. The head usher misses a week and asks one of the others to do the verse that week. Other people volunteer to bring a verse. Finally, some of them are enjoying the time so much they decide to start or join a small group.

When they started, the ushers thought they were just there to hand out pieces of paper and get people to sit down. With a process like this, it's likely God will help them move from serving out of a sense of obligation (or avoidance of singing during the service) to serving out of the overflow of their relationship with Him and each other. This is a step forward in their spiritual journey, moving them down the continuum. They are becoming better disciples.

Take a moment and think of everywhere men are involved in the church—in the sound booth, the praise team or choir, the youth programs,

Sunday school classes, the nursery, as parking lot attendees. How can you inspire leaders to reach these men where they are and help them become disciples of Jesus Christ?

EVERY MAN IS PART OF YOUR MEN'S MINISTRY

Finally, an all-inclusive men's ministry helps every man in the church feel like he is a part of something bigger than himself. It allows each man to be involved in your church wherever he feels God is calling him to participate.

If every man in the church is part of our men's ministry, then we must come up with innovative and effective ways to communicate that message to, well, every man! (This is why the *resonance* and *external slogan* concepts coming up in chapter 8 are so important.)

For instance, one church we have worked with calls their men's ministry *Iron Men*. To help every man feel a part of the men's ministry, they always refer to the men of the church as iron men. If you go to church there—even for one week—you are an iron man. Almost every time there is an announcement to the men, whether it is in the service or elsewhere, the statement is made, "Every man in our church is an iron man." Sounds hokey? Perhaps, but when you look around the sanctuary, you'll see the guys sit up a little straighter every time it is said.

Wherever men are involved, you need to "claim" them for your men's ministry in a way that supports and honors the other ministries of the church. Help these committed men understand that coming to the annual men's retreat or monthly men's breakfast or weekly Bible study is not a requirement to be part of the men's ministry. The men working with children need to see themselves as a man in ministry. Provide apron/smocks in the infant classes with the logo of your men's ministry. This gives a dual benefit. First of all, the man looks down at that logo and says, "The men of this church consider me a part of the men's ministry. They think what I am doing with kids is an important ministry. I've got the smock to prove it!" Second, the moms dropping off their children see the logo and say, "Wow, the men of this church are willing to do whatever it takes. They've even got guys working in the nursery!"

Help men who assist with parking see themselves as men in ministry. Give them prayer cards each Sunday with the men's ministry logo, a Scripture verse, and a prayer request for the church. Ask them to use any downtime to pray.

What other areas can you think of where men are already involved? How could you engage those men in discipleship and help them feel like they are part of the men's ministry in your church? Think about men who serve or participate in:

- Leading a boys Sunday school class
- Working in the sound booth
- Participating in a couples Sunday school class or small group
- Helping in the youth group
- Involved in the building project
- Singing in the choir or praise team
- Coaching a children's team in a sports league
- Working with the Boy Scout troop or Awana

There is no end to the creative and unique ways you can help men feel like they are a part of what God is doing through the men of your church. In the end, the message must communicate that it's not about a program that you want men to join. Help men feel like your church values and desires that every man would learn to experience God's love and the brotherhood of other men.

The goal of your ministry to men is to create a system that moves men from wide to deep across this continuum. You have in your arsenal every interaction your church has with every man. In the next chapters, we'll pull these concepts together into a system that moves the conveyor belt and connects these activities so that every man in your church can become a passionate disciple of Jesus Christ.

REMEMBER THIS

- No single activity can meet the needs of every man in your church. Where a man is in his spiritual journey will determine the kinds of offerings that appeal to him.

- Leaders need to agree on the target audience for a ministry activity or program.

- Having an all-inclusive ministry to men mind-set means:

    - Everything that your church does that touches a man is men's ministry. Everything.

    - The size of your men's ministry is equal to the total number of men in your church, plus every man you'd like to have in your church.

    - You should leverage the efforts of the other ministries to help you achieve your purpose of discipling men.

- Inspire other leaders in the church to see every interaction they have with men as a disciple-making opportunity.

- Give men who are working in other ministries something to identify them as part of the men's ministry, even though they may be working in the nursery, as an usher, or in the parking lot ministry.

Talk About This

1. Where are you on your spiritual journey? Take a few minutes for each person on your team to tell his story.

2. What group of men do you most feel drawn to disciple? What about the other men on your leadership team—do they seem to be drawn toward one type of man? What difference will this make in terms of where you focus your efforts as a leader?

3. Brainstorm some of the activities that men in your church are involved in that aren't "men's ministry." Does your church battle an "us versus them" attitude with these ministries? If so, what are some ways you can get beyond this?

4. List a few concrete steps your men's ministry can take to support the other ministries in the church. How could you help them disciple men more effectively? Is there an "unexpected leader" you could encourage with a vision for discipling men?

Pray About This

Pray together as a leadership team . . .

• that God would help every man in your church move forward in his spiritual journey.

• that God would help each of you find your calling—the unique way God has wired you to work with men—and maximize the impact you have with men.

• that the other ministries of the church see that the men's ministry is as committed to their success as it is to its own.

• that your pastor embraces the all-inclusive mind-set and comes to see their role as being the "tip of the spear" for your church's ministry to men.

PART THREE

PLANNING AND EXECUTING
YOUR MINISTRY TO MEN

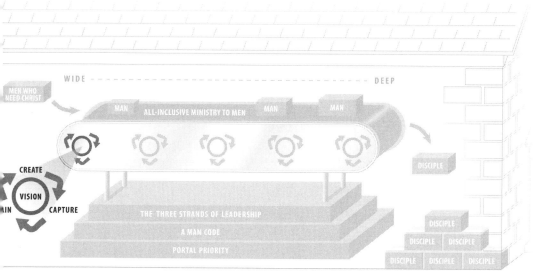

VISION:
A COMPELLING REASON FOR
MEN TO GET INVOLVED

Every conveyor belt has a motor that provides power to keep it moving. The power for your discipleship ministry with men is the Vision–Create–Capture–Sustain strategy. We'll deal with these concepts in the next four chapters of the book. We begin with helping you instill a sense of mission and vision in the men of your church.

WOULD YOU DO US A FAVOR? Tap your foot while you read this section of the book.

Seriously. This is not just an academic exercise where you will get the point even if you don't actually do what we say. We really want you to tap your foot while you read the next few pages of this book. Go ahead. Feel free to move it very slightly so that people around you don't think you're weird. Just make sure you tap your foot up and down. Are you tapping? Good.

If you stopped a man in your church on Sunday morning and asked why he was there, what would he say? You'd probably hear answers like, "Coming to church is the right thing to do"; "I want to make sure my family comes to church"; "I like to worship"; or, "I like the sermons." A particularly transparent man might say, "My wife wants me to come and I don't want to make her mad."

What about some of the men who are more involved? If you asked an usher why he served, how would he answer? How about a man who helps park cars? Sings on the praise team? Leads a men's small group? Works with the middle school youth group?

(Don't stop tapping your foot yet. Trust us.)

Too often men go to church without any real sense of purpose. They participate in activities because they are supposed to, or because someone asks them to, but they don't really know why they are involved. Most of them have never been given a compelling reason why the church should be a priority in their lives. They have never heard—in language they can relate to—that joining Christ in transforming the world is the adventure their hearts have always longed for.

For No Apparent Reason

Are you still tapping your foot? Let's assume this chapter kept going on and on and we never told you to stop. How long would you keep tapping? If you are a skeptical person, you might tap a few times and then quickly stop. If you are a particularly diligent person, you might keep tapping your foot for five or even ten minutes. But eventually every person who reads this book will stop. Why? Because you would realize you were tapping your foot for no good reason.

What if we said, "Tap your foot for ten minutes and we'll give you $10,000"? Almost any man would be willing to do that. Why? Because he understands the goal he is trying to accomplish. (We aren't giving you $10,000, so if you are still tapping your foot, you can stop now.)

Many men in churches are "tapping their feet" with no idea why. They may continue to be engaged for a while, but eventually they'll get tired, bored, and discouraged. And then their hearts will begin to grow cold, wither, and die.

These men know down deep inside that they were made for something more.

The Power of Vision

The first step in building the right strategy is to formulate your vision. God desires for the church to reach men with the gospel of Christ and help them grow to maturity. In the Great Commission (Matthew 28:18–20), Jesus calls us to make disciples by sharing His message. In Ephesians 4:11–13, Paul teaches that God gives some people special abilities to equip others for works of service. Leaders, then, are called to disciple and equip people so they can do the actual work of the ministry and mature to become all God is calling them to be.

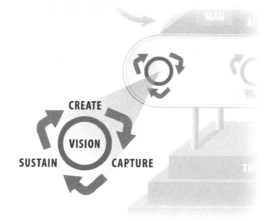

In the fourth century BC, Philip of Macedonia took control of several northern Greek cities. Down in Athens, the two greatest political orators of the day, Isocrates and Demosthenes, spoke out about the danger. They debated whether the men of Athens should attack Philip or wait and see if he attacked Athens. Isocrates, a teacher, made sure he presented the facts well. Demosthenes, on the other hand, concerned himself not only with what was "true," but also with what could be "made true" by the actions he advocated.

> ### THE **BIG** IDEA
>
> Ideas are more powerful than labor. Ideas set forces in motion that, once released, can no longer be contained.

Needed: More Demosthenes

Both men addressed the threat that Philip presented. When Isocrates finished explaining why they should wait, people commented: "How well he speaks!" But when Demosthenes spoke about Philip's threat, they exclaimed: "Let's march against Philip!"[1]

We need more "Demosthenes" in our interactions with the men in the church. We have cheated men by obscuring the incredible adventure of changing the world through Christ behind programs and activities.

Ideas are more powerful than labor. Ideas set forces in motion that, once released, can no longer be contained. Here are some examples of important ideas expressed in a powerful manner.

- "We will put a man on the moon by the end of the decade." —*John F. Kennedy*
- "A computer in every home and on every desk." —*Bill Gates*
- "I want to make it possible for anyone in the world to be able to taste a Coke during my lifetime." —*Robert Woodruff, CEO, the Coca-Cola Company, 1950s*

Do ideas make a difference? Today you can ascend to the top of the highest mountains in Nepal or descend to the lowest elevation on earth, Death Valley, and find, what? Empty Coke cans. Communicating the right idea in a compelling way is a powerful force.

If your announcements state that your "men's ministry will meet Saturday morning at 7:00 for breakfast and fellowship," that's a lie. It may be technically accurate, but it is a lie in every way that matters. Your men's ministry is not a meeting on some schedule of activities. Your men's ministry is about being part of what God is doing to transform the lives of men and women through the men of your church.

Men are tired of doing things "just because they should" or for no apparent reason. Men—especially younger men—want to be involved in something bigger than themselves.

MAKING IT RESONANT

If we said, "Just Do It," what images come to your mind? What about the slogan "Be All That You Can Be"? Both slogans work because the companies and organizations behind them have spent a tremendous amount of time, effort, and money reinforcing them to our hearts and minds. The words resonate with us.

Consider "Just Do It." There is nothing in those three words that mentions sports. The slogan could just have easily been adopted by a travel agency, a credit card company, or a job placement firm. But not anymore. Those words will now be owned forever by Nike.

Such phrases resonate with millions of people around the world. How about your men? Are you communicating with them in a way that connects with them emotionally? We need to go beyond simply conveying information to our men. In most cases they don't need more information;

they need God to awaken their hearts. Our job is to faithfully communicate in ways that stir the passion of our men for His glory.

A Process for Developing Your Vision

The vision for your men's ministry needs to be in line with the overarching vision and the particular purpose of your church.

Does your church have a purpose, mission, or vision statement? If so, write it in the space provided or on another sheet of paper.

_____

_____

_____

_____

_____

We will now help you formulate the vision of your men's ministry in three steps: as an *internal planning statement,* an *external slogan,* and an *elevator speech.*

Step One: An Internal Purpose Statement for Your Men's Ministry

Does your men's ministry have a vision or purpose statement? Let's take some time right now to review or formulate one by thinking through some of the key ideas that should be included. We call this an *internal purpose statement* because it should be used mainly with your leadership team as an aid in prayer and strategic planning.

Two of our foundational principles are particularly important as you think about the vision of your men's ministry. First, remember that *it takes a long time to make a disciple.* Have a long-term perspective. Don't look for a quick fix in a few months. Instead, pray and plan for what God wants to do over the next five or ten years.

Second, *most meaningful change takes place in the context of relationships.* Men change as their lives rub up against the lives of other men. Your men's ministry vision should include helping men develop meaningful relationships with other men.

You may want to have biblical themes and phrases reflected in your internal purpose statement. Consider the following Scripture passages (and others). Make notes of key ideas and themes that you would like to consider for your purpose statement: Proverbs 27:17; Matthew 28:18–20; Galatians 6:1–2;

Ephesians 4:11–16; Colossians 1:28–29; Colossians 3:19, 21; 2 Timothy 2:2.

_____

_____

_____

_____

Not only should you be aware of what the Bible teaches about ministering to men, you should also have a good handle on the practical needs of men in your church and community. It won't do you any good to design a men's ministry that won't actually reach any of your men.

Take a short break and spend about twenty minutes on the phone. Call one, two, or three representative men from your church and community. Discover their needs by asking questions such as the following:

- "In what area of your life do you feel the most pressure?"
- "If our church could do one thing for you, what would you want it to be?"
- "What is the most valuable experience you've had at the church in the last year?"
- "What is the worst experience you've had at church in the last year?"

Note their answers in the space provided.

_____

_____

_____

_____

_____

Now, prayerfully combine the thoughts and ideas generated by this material into an internal purpose statement for the men's ministry of your church. Remember, a purpose statement basically says _what_ you will do and _how_ will you do it.

Whatever words you use, your purpose should have at its heart Jesus' command to "make disciples."

Here's a sample men's ministry internal purpose statement: "To reach men with a credible offer of the gospel and equip them as transformational leaders for their families, church, work, and the world." (See appendix B for more vision statement examples.)

If your men's ministry has a purpose statement, write it here. If not, write a sentence that captures the essence of what you believe God wants the men's ministry of your church to accomplish.

_____

_____

_____

_____

_____

Step Two: An External Slogan to Challenge Your Men

Next, it is helpful to have a "call" or slogan that resonates with the men in your church. While your internal purpose statement charts a course, the *external slogan* helps recruit your team—its Demosthenes! It doesn't change or add to your purpose statement but rather "distills" it to a simple, high-impact message. It can help make the vision clear, even powerful, to your men. It's how Kennedy, Gates, and Woodruff captured people's imagination.

When men hear your slogan, you want them to remember the compelling ministry being accomplished for and by your men. A slogan is like a plastic bag at the grocery store. You don't go to the store to get a bag; the bag allows you to carry all your items home. A slogan or phrase that resonates is like an empty bag that you fill with the content and experiences that support the vision and mission of your church. After a few years, men who hear your slogan will automatically think about the incredible mission trip to Mexico, the amazing outreach event in your community, the day they reroofed the widow's house, or the way their group helped a man through his marriage crisis.

How will you call men to go with you on this adventure? Bruce Barton once said, "Jesus brought forth man's best efforts not with the promise of great reward, but of great obstacles."

Develop a resonant phrase or slogan that lets your men know you are playing for keeps. Call men to join a great vision of what God could do in your midst. Inspire them to join a cause that literally means the difference between eternal life and death for hundreds and thousands of men and their families.

Look for a short, visual, concrete, memorable statement that resonates with men. Make it action-oriented, rather than descriptive. Imagine what it was like for rural fishermen to hear Jesus' call to "make disciples of all nations" (Matthew 28:18–20)!

After attending our Leadership Training Center, one leader took his accurate, precise, and completely boring purpose statement and turned it into Training Men for the Battle. The Lord has used this (and other truths he learned) to give new power for his ministry to men.

Here are some sample slogans: Building Iron Men; Brothers in the Great Adventure; Every Man a Disciple; Reaching Men, Exalting Christ. See Appendix B for more examples.

Use the space below to try out several slogans, then provisionally pick the best one.

_____

_____

_____

_____

In addition, many leaders have found it helpful to have a resonant name for their men's ministry. The right name gives your ministry an identity that is compelling and inviting. Here are some sample names: Men of Faith; Iron Men; Band of Brothers; Men of Valor. (Once again, additional ideas can be found in appendix B.)

Use the space below to brainstorm names. Try them out with your slogan. For example: "Men of Faith—Brothers in the Great Adventure." (You'll finalize your name, slogan, and internal purpose statement in the exercises in chapter 12.)

_____

_____

_____

_____

_____

Step Three: Your Elevator Speech

Train your leaders to share their passion for your men's ministry with other men. Help them develop a four- or five-sentence explanation about why they are excited about what God is doing through the men of your church.

This is called an "elevator speech." Imagine you are getting on an elevator and one of the men from your church walks on as the doors are closing. He says hello and then asks, "I know you are involved in the men's ministry at church, and I've been thinking, why should I get more involved?" He then pushes the button for the fifth floor and you have less than a minute to convince him. What will you say?

Begin training your leaders to give their elevator speech by working on a short script that contains:

- *The Introduction.* For example, "Eddie, I'd love to quickly share with you what God is doing in our ministry to men."
- *The Vision.* "As you may know, we are training men for the battle. Nothing has the power to change the world like reaching men . . ."
- *A Success Story.* "I don't know if you've met Jose Aguilar yet, but he has a great testimony of how God is working. Ted Rogers invited him to our outreach lunch last fall and Jose joined a small group. One of the other men led him to Christ, and now Jose and his wife have joined our church. It fires me up to think that his three precious children have a whole new future ahead of them with a godly dad."
- *A Next Step.* "We have some great ministries going on right now—small groups, service projects, and our annual retreat. Also, if you'd like to sit in on one of our leadership meetings, we'd love to have you join us as our guest. Our next meeting is a week from Sunday. Would you like to come?"

Here's a real-life example. Brett had invited a man to join his men's ministry leadership team. After the first meeting, Brett's friend expressed doubt about whether he wanted to be involved. It seemed like meetings and activities. What was the men's ministry really trying to accomplish?

They had both just witnessed a man in their small group who abandoned his wife and teenaged kids for another woman. Brett was ready with an elevator speech:

"Bill, do you remember what happened with Rob? You and I sat next to him for six months in our small group. Did you have any idea something was going on?"

"No," he said sadly. "I didn't."

"Me neither. And that's why we need a men's ministry. Because every man in our church needs another man who can look him in the eye and tell when something's wrong."

In a flash, Bill "got it." He literally slammed his hand down on the table. "I want to be a part of that!"

Take a few minutes and write an elevator speech that quickly explains your vision for men's ministry in your church in the space below. Use the "Introduction, Vision, Success Story, Next Step" outline. Time your presentation to make sure you can tell the story in about sixty seconds.

_____

_____

_____

_____

_____

_____

_____

_____

_____

_____

Share your elevator speech with other men as often as you can. Have your emcees use their version at each of your events. Use it when you invite men to participate in activities, events, or groups. Use it when you meet potential leaders. Keep your vision in front of as many men as possible as much as possible.

BE VISION-FOCUSED
RATHER THAN EVENT-CENTERED

An external slogan helps you constantly remind your men that you are doing things for a reason. Too often, local church men's ministries have been driven by events rather than vision. We schedule events—like a monthly men's breakfast or annual retreat—and before long men perceive that the events are the ministry. We become discouraged when men don't attend events because that is how we measure the effectiveness of our ministry. Yet, often men don't come because there doesn't seem to be any larger purpose to the events.

If we are not careful, we can "begin" without really knowing where we want to "end." It is easy to get caught up in the breakneck pace of men's ministry and "event" yourself to mediocrity.

Every event that you schedule as a part of your ministry to men should serve your overall vision. At the event, explicitly communicate to the men how this event fits in the larger context of your ministry and the vision of the church. Explain what you hope to accomplish and how it contributes to your overall goals. Use your external slogan over and over to reinforce this vision.

BE POSITIVE, NOT NEGATIVE

Men want to respond to a challenge. They don't want to be yelled at. Make sure you formulate a vision with a positive agenda about what God can do rather than a negative rebuke about how bad men are doing. Men don't respond well when we talk down to them. Use a positive approach to draw men toward the great calling God has given them rather than berate them to leave lesser things behind.

It would be impossible for us to overemphasize the importance of developing and sharing the vision for your men's ministry (using the internal purpose statement, external slogan, and elevator speech). It is the single most important ingredient for creating the kind of atmosphere God uses to change men's hearts.

Most men today feel bored and left out of their churches. They are tapping their feet. Are your men tapping theirs? Why not call them to something great and see how they respond?

REMEMBER THIS

- Men are tired of doing things "just because they should" or for no apparent reason. Men want to be involved in something bigger than themselves.

- Your vision should be a resonant call to action, a compelling challenge, and a promise men will go someplace worthwhile.

- Your vision for the men's ministry has three components:

  - **An internal purpose statement.** This answers what you will do and how you will do it.

  - **An external slogan.** This is the public face of your men's ministry and should make men say, "I want to be a part of that!"

  - **An elevator speech.** Every leader should be equipped with a sixty-second explanation of the vision of the men's ministry, why a man would want to be involved, and an invitation to do something.

- Every event that you schedule as part of your ministry to men should serve your overall vision. If it doesn't, cancel it.

TALK ABOUT THIS

1. Men want to be a part of something going somewhere. How have you been frustrated in the past by being part of a group that seemed to lack direction and vision?

2. Are you presenting the men of your church with an opportunity to belong to something bigger than themselves? Think of the last few events your church held for men. Did you place those events in the context of a larger vision? Did you communicate that larger vision to men when you announced or invited men to the activity? How can you improve this for upcoming activities?

3. On a flip chart or whiteboard, draft or refine your men's ministry internal purpose statement based on input from your pastor and each other. Use the work you did while reading this chapter. Draft an internal statement as a group and write it in the space below.

_____

_____

_____

_____

_____

4. Effectively calling men to participate in the discipleship process will require you to capture their attention and challenge them to grow. Pick one of your slogans, fine-tune it, and write the statement in the space below. Then pick your ministry name and do the same thing with it. Take some time to discuss how you will use it.

_____

_____

_____

5. Allow each man on your leadership team to share his elevator speech. Make suggestions for how you can begin to share these with other men.

Pray About This

Pray together as a leadership team...

- that God would inspire your team and give you a compelling vision for your men.

- for guidance as you develop tools to communicate this vision.

- that God would help men clearly see the great adventure of following Jesus Christ.

CREATE MOMENTUM
BY PROVIDING VALUE

After you've defined a vision and begun to communicate it consistently, how do you get men to start moving on their spiritual journey? The key to help a stationary man get moving is to create value for him. Know your men, then reach them in ways that are relevant to their lives. This chapter will help you know how to effectively create momentum with all your men.

ONE BENEFIT OF LIVING in central Florida is our proximity to Cape Canaveral, where they launch the space shuttle. It's pretty amazing to see this mammoth machine strapped to external rocket boosters and a huge fuel tank, sitting on its tail pointed toward the sky. The voices of the controllers are calm and measured as they tick off checkpoints on the countdown to zero.

"Ignition!" Steam starts to escape and then smoke starts billowing. The shuttle shudders for a moment or two and then—barely perceptibly—it begins to lift off the pad.

At first it moves so slowly, you almost expect it to fall over. After all, once it leaves the ground, it's basically sitting on the hot gases from the rocket engines. And then, "The shuttle has cleared the tower." Now it is definitely going up, moving faster and faster. Within minutes, it is traveling 17,000 miles per hour. From a hundred miles away, spectators can see the bright flame as it rises in an arc toward orbit.

The shuttle's external fuel tank is enormous. It holds 500,000 gallons of rocket fuel, which all burns up in about five minutes. Then the shuttle travels another four million miles on a little bucket of fuel.

The greatest amount of energy required in nature is that amount required to overcome inertia and put a stationary object—like a space shuttle—into motion. Overcoming spiritual inertia is the same way. We are surrounded by men who are spiritually stationary.

Two Common Traits of Men

Men exhibit two traits: Some are busy, and some are tired. Most are both!

There is a tremendous volume of noise in our lives. We live in a world of fast career tracks, high-speed Internet connections, and easy credit. All week long men are being bombarded by the media, their coworkers, their boss, their family—everybody wants something.

No wonder men rarely take time for spiritual self-examination. Many attend church only out of obligation, if at all. Others invest themselves in church hoping to feel needed and successful. See if you recognize either of these hypothetical men:

John attends church because he feels it is something he should do for his family. His wife really wants him to go to church, and he agrees with her that it is a good idea for his kids to receive some moral and religious instruction. He goes through the motions—attending worship services, sending the kids to Sunday school, putting an envelope in the offering plate—but he's not actively pursuing a relationship with Jesus Christ. So he goes, but mostly to watch, not participate. John is a tourist at church: He enjoys the experience while he's there, but then he goes home and life gets back to normal.

Frank, on the other hand, loves church. It makes him feel needed, like he is making a contribution. He attends faithfully every Sunday and serves on several committees and boards. He keeps saying he'd like to be more involved with men, but he's not in a small group nor does he seem to have any true friends in the church. When he's invited to join the men's Sunday school class or go on the retreat, he regretfully declines because he's "too busy."

John and Frank are both cultural Christians. Even though they look different from the outside, on the inside they are virtually identical. They are spiritually stationary. They are focused on themselves. A huge challenge for leaders is to get guys like John and Frank out of the comfortable patterns they use to stiff-arm God. (Of course, we face just as big a challenge with guys we would like to attract who aren't in our church at all.)

Ironically, both John and Frank would likely respond if presented with a compelling challenge.

Discipleship is a spiritual journey, and as the saying goes, "A journey of a thousand miles begins with the first step." So how do we get men to take that first step—or for some, the next step—in this spiritual journey? In the last chapter we discussed step one, clearly communicating a compelling vision for your men's ministry. What's next?

OFFERING SOMETHING OF VALUE

Engage a man's attention by offering him something he will find valuable. Tired men need to believe that getting involved will be worth the effort. Busy men need to believe that of all the opportunities clamoring for their time, the one you are offering them is top notch. In short, you have to show them the value of getting involved.

When you create value with an activity, you create momentum, the first gear that propels the conveyor belt of your discipleship process.

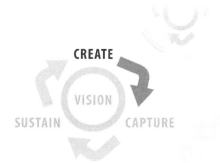

Often, we provide value for men with some kind of experience or activity: a Promise Keepers conference, the men's retreat, a men's rally, or a barbecue. But it doesn't have to be a big event. Often, the most valuable thing to a man is some personal one-on-one time, like inviting him to breakfast or lunch. Look for anything that compels a man to take a step forward in his spiritual journey.

There is no shortage of activities for men today. A little analysis will give you the insights you need to get your men's attention. You'll need to answer these two questions:

- What types of men are we trying to reach?
- What kinds of things will interest them?

KNOW YOUR MEN: FIVE TYPES

As you devise a strategy to create momentum among your men, you will want to take some time to categorize the men in your church—perhaps by age or life situation. Below is Man in the Mirror's typology that many churches use to help target their efforts. Every man in your church fits into one or more of the following five categories:

Type 1: Men who *need* a relationship with *Christ*—Romans 6:23; 1 John 5:11–12

Type 2: Men who are *cultural Christians* (men on the "fringe")—Matthew 13:22

Type 3: Men who are *biblical Christians*, or want to be—Matthew 13:23

Type 4: Men who are *leaders,* or want to be—2 Timothy 2:2

Type 5: Men who are *hurting*—Galatians 6:2

Type 1: Men Who Need Christ

These are men who are not Christians and know they aren't. Most don't go to church. You will need to reach outside of the church to pull these men in.

Take a few moments to think of men connected to your church who may not know Christ. What do these men look like?

- A man who comes occasionally with his family—think Mother's Day or Easter
- A neighbor or coworker someone brought to the men's BBQ or Super Bowl party
- Guys who play on the church softball team or show up for "Friday night basketball" in your church gym
- A man who comes to the Christmas play or the Easter cantata

Picture these men in your mind. Write down their names. How would you describe them?

_____

_____

_____

_____

_____

Type 2: Men Who Are Cultural Christians

These men come in two flavors: John and Frank (from our story earlier in the chapter). If you are a leader, these are the guys who probably frustrate you the most. They often seem poised to get involved, telling you what you want to hear, but then backing out at the last second.

John is typical of men on the fringe of the church. He may attend services fairly regularly, but isn't involved much beyond that.

There are many men either just inside or outside the doors of the church. Biblically, these men have let the worries of this life and the deceitfulness of money choke the Word and make it unfruitful (Matthew 13:22); they've let the yeast of culture work through the whole batch of dough (Galatians 5:9); they've done that which is permissible but not beneficial (1 Corinthians 6:12); they're high risk for a great crash because they built on sand and not the rock (Matthew 7:24–27).

Frank, on the other hand, is very involved, but he uses his busyness at the church to keep others at arm's length. He may at one time have had a vibrant faith, but the work of the church has overwhelmed his love for Christ (Revelation 2:2–4). Many people know who Frank is, but nobody really knows Frank.

The only way we've seen men like John and Frank be reached is through other men who take a personal interest in their lives. This can be difficult, because Frank will likely brush you off the first few times. Don't get annoyed. Just keep trying. Eventually, when they're ready, they will open the door to a deeper relationship. Make sure someone is there to take advantage of the opportunity!

Picture these men in your mind. What are their names? Describe them in your own words.

_____

_____

_____

_____

_____

Type 3: Men Who Are Biblical Christians

These men are the "bread and butter" of your ministry. These guys, especially those early in their spiritual journey, are eager to develop their faith. Some are actively engaged, others are waiting for someone to show them what to do.

Three things have special appeal to these types of men: learning, serving, and leading. First, they learn by responding to opportunities to study the Bible and develop their faith. That's why these men fill small groups and Sunday school classes. Second, once biblical Christians get a taste of serving—at the homeless shelter or doing yard work for a widow, for instance—they often get turned on and will keep coming back. Finally, these are your candidates to begin exploring leadership. They'll join an officer training class or be willing to fill in for a missing usher or a sick Sunday school teacher.

It is easy to take these men for granted. After all, they pretty much do what you ask them to. They respond to the announcements, sign up at the table outside the sanctuary, and show up for the work project on Saturday morning. Of course, they make up a much higher percentage of the guys who show up for men's activities. But beware: You must challenge these men to keep growing. Bored men—even biblical Christians—are easy targets for distraction and sin. Be on the lookout for men who are "tapping their feet."

Are there specific men that came to mind as you read about biblical Christians? Picture these men in your mind. What are their names? Describe them in your own words.

_____

_____

_____

_____

_____

Type 4: Men Who Are Leaders

Right now you're probably thinking, *Oh boy, do I wish we had more leaders!* You may have more than you think. A leader is anyone who takes responsibility to get something done and influences others to join him in the effort. Once a man begins to be concerned about reaching and discipling other men, he has become a leader.

The men on your ministry teams and committees are leaders, of course. The guys who lead small groups and teach Sunday school classes are obviously leaders as well. But so is the head usher, the captain of the softball team, the youth worker who mentors a boy with no dad, the man who sets up chairs each week, and other unseen and unexpected leaders.

You may think you don't really need to create value for these men. "They're already involved. They've bought into what the church is trying to do." Yes, but they are often busy and tired too. These men need you to consistently help them remember why they got involved in the first place.

Who are the leaders in your church? Write down the names of the "expected" and the "unexpected" leaders. How would you describe these men? Are they excited? Tired? What do they need?

Type 5: Men Who Are Hurting

Regardless of their spiritual maturity, all men go through difficulties at various times in their lives. At any given point, as many as half the men in your church may be going through marital problems, financial issues, struggling with a wayward child, involvement with Internet porn, dealing with the loss of a job, or struggling with the health crisis of a loved one.

What are the two or three most significant issues facing your hurting men? Could these men get help in your church? Make sure you are supporting men in a way that makes it realistic for them to ask for help. There was once an actual announcement in a church bulletin that went something like this: "Men, are you struggling with feelings of depression because of financial or marriage problems? Sometimes it helps just to have someone to talk to. Call our counseling center to make a confidential appointment today at

555-1234. Ask for Susan." While this is a great announcement telling guys that it's OK to ask for help, very few men will call a stranger named Susan.

Remember the statistics from chapter 2? Of the 108 million men in America, 66 million make no profession of faith in Jesus Christ. This means over 60 percent of men need Christ. Of the 42 million men who do make some kind of profession of faith in Christ, only an estimated six million are involved in any kind of ongoing spiritual development (one out of seven). This means that about 36 million men in America are cultural Christians. The six million biblical Christians are an estimated 5.5 percent of the general population. In our experience, something like 20 percent of biblical Christians are leaders (see Figure 8).

LEVEL OF SPIRITUAL DEVELOPMENT AMONG AMERICAN MEN		
	NUMBER IN U.S.	PERCENTAGE OF ALL MEN
Men who need Christ	66 million	61%
Cultural Christians	36 million	33%
Biblical Christians	5 million	5.5%
Leaders	1 million	<1%

SOURCES: The Barna Group, www. barna.org; Man in the Mirror Leadership Training Conferences, Orlando, Florida.

Figure 8

In our Training Center classes, we ask men to consider the proportion of these groups in their church. We've included the basic range of answers in the table below. What about your church? Estimate your own numbers, both in percentages and in real numbers. At the end of the chapter, you'll use this information to evaluate your current efforts to reach men.

LEVEL OF SPIRITUAL DEVELOPMENT IN OUR CHURCH			
OUR CHURCH:	# OF MEN	%	SAMPLE CHURCHES
Men who need Christ	_____	_____	1–15%
Cultural Christians	_____	_____	35–70%
Biblical Christians	_____	_____	10–40%
Leaders	_____	_____	5–15%

Figure 9

THE FIVE TYPES OF MEN ACROSS THE CONTINUUM

Let's take a look back at the wide-deep continuum from chapter 2. If you were to place each type of man across the continuum at the point that best describes him, it would look like this:

Type 1:	Type 2:	Type 3:	Type 4:
NEED CHRIST	**CULTURAL CHRISTIANS**	**BIBLICAL CHRISTIANS**	**LEADERS**

WIDE   DEEP

Note: Type 5: Hurting men are in each of the other four groups.

The wide-deep continuum serves as a metaphor for a man's spiritual development. As a man moves forward in his spiritual journey toward Christ, he moves down this continuum as well.

The continuum is a helpful planning tool. There is no such thing as a one-size-fits-all men's activity. It's important to take into account what group of men you are trying to reach with any event you are planning for your men.

Choosing Activities Across the Continuum

Figure 10 shows a continuum drawn with the four types of men labeled so that it forms four columns. (Remember, there are hurting men in each category.) The chart is entitled "Men's Ministry Activities by Type." Under each type of man, make a list of the kinds of activities you think each type of men might enjoy. To get you started, we've put in several examples. Add your own ideas in the blanks provided.

MEN'S MINISTRY ACTIVITIES BY TYPE			
Type 1: **NEED CHRIST**	Type 2: **CULTURAL CHRISTIANS**	Type 3: **BIBLICAL CHRISTIANS**	Type 4: **LEADERS**
WIDE			DEEP
Sports/Outdoor Activities	Seminar	Retreat	Officer Training
Daddy-Daughter Dance	Sunday School	Small Group	Accountability Groups
	Service Project	Mission Trip	

Figure 10

Managing Your Expectations

The continuum can also help you manage expectations. One year, a church of about eight hundred invited Man in the Mirror to conduct a *Success That Matters* seminar. Over 120 men attended the seminar. The follow-up was very well received, and the seminar created a lot of momentum.

The next year, they did another seminar, and this time Brett was called on to conduct *Leading a Mission Driven Life.* Brett arrived and met with the leadership team, who were a little downcast. They only had seventy-five men registered for the event and couldn't figure out why. But things were better than they thought.

Brett drew a picture of the continuum on a whiteboard, and after a brief explanation of the types of men, asked the leaders how many of their men fit into each group. He wrote their answers on a whiteboard. They determined that of the about 350 men in their church, 230 either needed Christ or were cultural Christians; the remaining 120 were either biblical Christians or leaders.

Then Brett explained that the *Success That Matters* seminar is targeted for those guys who need Christ or are on the fringe. The marketing material focuses on men trying to balance work, marriage, kids, hobbies, finances, and recreational interests. It asks the question, "Have you ever thought, 'There's got to be more to life than this'?" Out of the 120 men who attended that event, about 80 men needed Christ or were cultural Christians. The other 40 were biblical Christians or leaders.

But *Leading a Mission Driven Life* is targeted more toward biblical Christians and leaders. On the continuum, *Success That Matters* falls closer to the wide side; *Mission Driven Life* falls farther to the deep side. So the seventy-five men coming to the current seminar represented over half of the target group for this event! In other words, even though the total number in attendance was lower, the percentage of men in the target group was actually higher.

At the end of the meeting, the chart looked something like this:

800 PEOPLE AND 350 MEN			
Type 1: **NEED CHRIST** 5%=20 men	Type 2: **FRINGE/CULTURAL** 60%=210 men	Type 3: **BIBLICAL CHRISTIANS** 25%=85 men	Type 4: **LEADERS** 10%=35 men
WIDE			DEEP
Total of 230 out of 350 men		**Total of 120 out of 350 men**	
YEAR ONE **"Success That Matters"** Target: Fringe Attendance: 120 men Number in target audience: 80 Approx. 25% of the primary target audience		**YEAR TWO** **"Leading a Mission Driven Life"** Target: Biblical Christians/Leaders Attendance: 75 men, almost all biblical Christians /leaders Over 50% of the primary target audience	

The *Leading a Mission Driven Life* event reached a higher percentage of the target market. In other words, it may have been unrealistic to expect 120 men at the *Leading a Mission Driven Life*—and perhaps they should have had even more men the previous year! This analysis helped them manage their expectations about how many men should come to an activity. It could help you too.

IF YOU WANT MEN TO COME,
YOU HAVE TO ASK THEM

Get ready. You are about to read a foolproof "marketing plan" to get the men of your church to come to your next event. Ready? Here it is: First, create a four-color flyer for your event with cutting-edge graphics and hand it out to every man. Then make an animated PowerPoint presentation to show on the screen before every service starting two months before the event. You'll need to run some radio advertisements on the local Christian stations. Next, go out and purchase at least one billboard on every major artery leading to your church to advertise your event. Go to the local airfield and pay for a skywriter so that the week before your event men can look up and see "Men's BBQ Next Friday ☺" written in the sky. Finally, slip your pastor a Starbucks gift certificate to announce it from the pulpit. Everybody knows that if the pastor tells men what to do, they'll do it.

OK, so by now you've realized that the plan above is not only a little expensive but probably not effective either. It's just a formula for getting the guys to come who were going to attend anyway.

The Power of a Personal Invitation

If you want new men to come, you must add one strategy to your promotions: *personal invitations*. All of your flyers, announcements, and PowerPoint slides accomplish one thing: They make it more likely that a man will say yes *when someone asks him to go.*

It makes sense, doesn't it? Think about how most men come to Christ: most don't drive down the street, see one of those "God billboards," and go, "Wow. I need to ask Jesus Christ to be my Lord and Savior." No, someone spent time explaining the gospel to them, and then asked them if they would like to accept Christ.

According to surveys by Religion in American Life, only 2 or 3 percent of people attended church because of advertising, while 85 percent went after being invited by a friend or relative. Men need to be invited—personally. They will come to something with a friend they would never go to alone.

David is on the leadership team at his church. The team decided to host several events to build community among their men. The first was a father and child activity day. They put announcements in the bulletin, sent e-mails, even had the pastor mention it from the front. And when Saturday came, the leadership team gathered to greet and serve the men and children coming.

From Zero to Fifty

They waited. They waited some more. In the end, besides themselves, exactly nobody—zero men—came. (David was thinking about applying to *The Guinness Book of World Records* for the least successful church men's event.)

THE BIG IDEA

Give men what they need in the context of what they want.

The next event was scheduled to be a bowling night in January. Though a bit dispirited, they decided to go through with their plan. One of the leaders had suggested making the bowling night a competition. They recruited eleven captains who were each responsible for inviting four other men to be on their team. The night of the event, fifty-four men showed up, the most they had ever had for this type of men's activity. (They gave bonus pins for team members who did not attend church regularly—and had eleven unchurched men at the event.)

Why did it work? They only had to sign up eleven men for the event, then those eleven went out and personally recruited the other forty-three. If you want men to come, personally invite them.

GIVE MEN WHAT THEY NEED IN THE CONTEXT OF WHAT THEY WANT

How do you do reach men on the fringe without being "preachy"?

One Bible teaching model is, "What do men need to do?" Man in the Mirror's model has been, "What do men need *that they are willing to do?*" In other words, if a man needs to consider twenty areas, but he is only far enough along in his spiritual pilgrimage to engage in three of those areas, it doesn't make sense to talk about the other seventeen. Instead, focus on the three, lead him along, then add other subjects as he grows.

Most nominally committed men will be focused, at least initially, on only their felt needs—career, money, family, time management, and so on. That's okay. Talk to them about money, and show them what Jesus has to say about it. In other words, give men what they need in the context of what they want.

Because our message is based upon the truth of Scripture, we must be relevant while never compromising what is real. Francis Schaeffer said,

"Each generation of the church in each setting has the responsibility of communicating the gospel in understandable terms, considering the language and thought-forms of that setting."[1] We must speak God's truth to men in a language they can understand.

For instance, if you are trying to reach men who need Christ, inviting them to a thirty-six-week Bible study on the spiritual disciplines is probably not going to work. On the other hand, you can't expect your men to grow if all you offer is sports events and barbeques.

Some Final Guidelines

When you are working with men—at any level of spiritual maturity—a good rule is: Don't trick them! Don't use fun-sounding activities to attract guys, and then get superspiritual with them. This is what cult deprogrammers do, not men who want to reach other men for Christ.

Here are some other guidelines for activities that will attract men who need Christ and men on the fringe:

DO	DON'T
• Have events focused on felt needs: finances, marriage, career, recreation.	• Rely solely on events focused on purely spiritual needs: prayer, fasting, quiet time.
• Incorporate recreation or hobbies: sports, cars, movies.	• Incorporate activities that will make nonbelievers overly uncomfortable: long prayers, singing ten worship songs in a row, "hellfire and brimstone" speakers, or holding hands.
• Advertise honestly: Yes, it's at a church. Yes, we will talk about God at some point. Yes, we will make it fun and engaging.	• Bait and switch: "Before we play basketball, we have a short, thirty-five-minute evangelistic film we'd like to show you."
• Have fun.	• Make men feel guilty.
• Make it easy and natural for men to begin to develop relationships.	• Ignore the new guy or create contrived exercises to make men talk.
• Give them the "next step": Invite them back for something else.	• Make them have to figure out what they should do next if they are interested.
• Make men want to come back.	• Drive them away by being too "churchy."
• Think long-term, low pressure.	• Forget it takes a long time to make a disciple.

For more specific ideas on activities to reach the different types of men, turn to appendix C: "Creating Momentum for the Five Types of Men."

Many churches do a pretty good job of creating momentum. The next chapter will help you make sure these activities move men closer to Christ rather than just becoming another emotionally satisfying experience. To keep men moving spiritually, one idea makes all the difference: It is absolutely essential that in every instance we capture the momentum we create.

REMEMBER THIS

- Often the biggest challenge we face is to get guys out of the comfortable patterns they use to stiff-arm God.

- In order for men to choose to be involved in a discipleship activity, we must convince them of the value.

- It can be helpful to think of five types of men: men who need Christ; men who are cultural Christians; men who are biblical Christians; men who are leaders; and men who are hurting.

- To provide value, meet men where they are. Different activities appeal to different types of men.

- Personal invitations are the key to getting men to attend. All of your promotional efforts will only make it more likely they will say yes when someone asks them.

- Give men what they need in the context of what they want.

Talk About This

1. When was the last time you did something positive outside of your "comfort zone"? What caused you to take that step? How can this help as you consider how to get new men involved?

2. Think of the last big event you did for men. Which group of men did it focus on? Did the event help you achieve your purpose? How did people find out about the event? Were men personally invited by other men to attend?

3. Think about the men in your church who are cultural Christians. What are some things that might get those men off the spiritual sidelines and into the game?

4. As a team, use the continuum chart on the next page to compile the work you did earlier in the chapter. Write the types of men across the top and the estimated percentages in your church. Under the line, write down the activities your church does now—whether or not they are for men only—placing them at the approximate point on the continuum to represent the group(s) of men they reach.

5. Consider the percentage of each type of men in your church. Are there groups you are "overtargeting"? Are there groups of men in your church that your current efforts are missing? How could you adjust what you are doing now to help reach all of the men in your church?

Pray About This

Pray together as a leadership team . . .

• that men in your church would realize their need for God and would see your discipleship programs as a way to pursue Him.

• for each of the five different types of men in your church, think of a few men in each category and pray for them by name.

• for God to give you leaders with a heart for men at each stage of their spiritual journey.

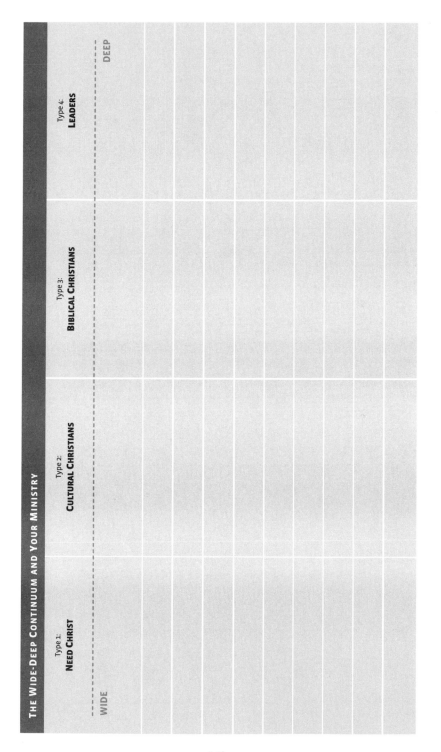

The Wide-Deep Continuum and Your Ministry

WIDE

Type 1:
NEED CHRIST

Type 2:
CULTURAL CHRISTIANS

Type 3:
BIBLICAL CHRISTIANS

Type 4:
LEADERS

DEEP

Capture Momentum With the Right Next Step

Many churches struggle with a roller coaster men's ministry. An event attracts new men. Four months later, the leadership team is wondering where they all went. This chapter covers the two mistakes in retaining new men, and gives practical hints on how to move men consistently forward toward authentic discipleship.

HAVE YOU EVER heard a story like this?

"We had an amazing men's retreat last year. This speaker came in and really challenged the guys. He shared how his relationship with his father was pretty bad and how that affected him as an adult. He told about his own failures and how God had restored him. He really connected with our men. Guys were getting emotional; groups of men were praying together about their relationships with their own sons and hurts from their relationships with their fathers. We had guys recommitting their lives to Christ. It was great."

Pause . . . "But most of the guys who went are no more involved in our church now than before the event. What happened to all those guys who were praying and crying together? Maybe they were just caught up in the emotion. In fact, I'm wondering if some of the guys had authentic experiences at all."

Or perhaps your story is more like this one: "Five years ago, there was a big men's event in town. We rented a bus and ninety-three guys signed up. It was awesome! Then three years ago, it was a little bit longer drive and during a bad weekend, so we only got fifty guys to go. Last year it was local again, and we thought we'd get a bunch of guys to go. But we struggled to get twenty-three guys signed up. We ended up going in a few cars and it just wasn't the same."

Then come the reasons: "The pastor didn't really support it from the pulpit." "It was a bad weekend because of (insert sporting event here)." "A lot of guys feel like they've 'been there, done that.'"

A Roller Coaster Men's Ministry

At a meeting of the National Coalition of Men's Ministries, Pastor Sid Woodruff shared a great illustration about riding a roller coaster at a theme park. Living in central Florida, we know a few things about theme park rides. So we're going to amplify on Sid's roller coaster metaphor.

Imagine climbing in the newest roller coaster with a great sense of anticipation. The shoulder harness comes down and you feel a little shot of adrenaline. You look ahead at the drop that's coming and realize you can't embarrass yourself by climbing out at the last minute like a scared little girl—especially since there are little girls on the roller coaster too, and they don't look all that scared.

You rumble out of the start house, go around a corner, and start up a steep incline. Click, click, click . . . You get about a quarter of the way up, just far enough for all the cars to be suspended vertically, barely clinging to the track, and then you stop. Is it broken? Did someone read the terror on your face and decide to show you mercy?

No.

Over loudspeakers you hadn't noticed before, a countdown begins. At 0, you are catapulted up toward the sky. As you approach the top of the hill, you quickly ask God to take care of your children and wife, then try to decide if you want to die with your eyes open or shut.

The bottom drops out, or rather, you are snatched back down again. The laws of physics have been overcome! The roller coaster didn't leave the tracks! Now, the ride really begins. You are yanked around hairpin corners, shot up inclines, dropped down into metallic ravines, and flipped upside down a few times for good measure.

What was terrifying soon turns into fun. The sights of the theme park shooting by, the sound of the others on the ride yelling and screaming with delight, your own joy as you realize, "I'm not going to die." A few more bone-wrenching corners, and then comes an upside-down, twisty-turny flip inspired by the double helix structure of DNA. You hear yourself shouting with glee, "Is that all you got? You can do better than that!" And then you come around the corner and . . . you stop.

You're back in the little starting house again. The ride operators are looking at you with the same disinterested stares they had when you left. There's another mass of expectant park guests waiting to take your seat on the ride. As you stand up and climb out, you look back and realize:

I'm getting off the ride exactly where I got on. I really haven't gone anywhere.

This story contains many parallels to men's ministry. The big event, the adventure retreat, the altar call. Done correctly, these events can catapult your ministry forward. But, too often, several months or even a year or two later, leaders look around after these events and realize their ministry is right back where they started. Instead of having a men's ministry that grows, albeit through peaks and valleys, their men's ministry stagnates. They are not able to capture and sustain the momentum. They have a roller coaster men's ministry.

If you were to make a chart of this kind of men's ministry, it might look something like this:

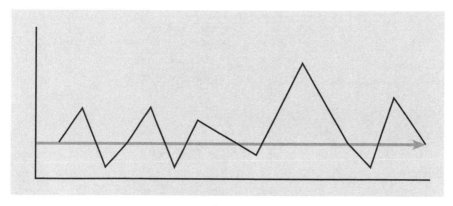

Figure 11
Typical Roller Coaster Men's Ministry

What about your ministry to men? Are you so frustrated that you're ready to shout, "Stop this ride! I want to get off!"? Can you identify more with the valleys than the peaks? Does your men's ministry feel like a series of highs— great men's events, experiences, revivals—while there's no real difference today in the spiritual commitment of your men? Have you seen a substantial increase in the number of men who are actively pursuing discipleship from a year ago or five years ago? If you don't like your answers, you can get off the roller coaster and start taking your men toward a new destination.

Two Traps in Men's Ministry

But before you can get off the roller coaster, you have to know how you got on in the first place. If a roller coaster men's ministry is the problem, what's the cause? In our experience, there are two different traps that men's ministries fall into.

Trap #1: The Personality-Driven Men's Ministry

Some churches have men's ministries that go extremely well for a couple of years and then run out of steam. They have several great events each year, ongoing small groups for men, big groups going to Promise Keepers, well-attended mission trips . . . you get the picture.

But then, over the course of several months, it all just seems to die out. The next men's retreat comes around and it's not very well organized. Only half as many guys show up as last year. Small groups are disappearing, and the guy in charge of them seems to have lost interest. Generally, activities just sort of fade away.

This is the classic symptom of a personality-driven men's ministry. In this scenario a dynamic, spiritually mature leader gathers a group of men around him and organizes the men's ministry. He has the respect of his pastor and the leadership of the church, and they give him the resources he needs to make things happen. His organizational skills help ensure high quality events that guys appreciate.

Unfortunately, one day this leader gets a promotion that requires additional travel. And his right-hand man has to reduce his involvement when his mother faces a health crisis and has to move in with him. They haven't recruited any additional leaders, so there's no one else ready or willing to step up. It's like someone taking their foot off the gas as the car speeds down the road. It keeps going for a while on sheer momentum. But soon it will coast to a stop.

Trap #2: The Event-Driven Men's Ministry

Perhaps your men's ministry goes through a series of ups and downs several times throughout each year: You spend a couple of months hyping the

Big Men's Rally and BBQ right after Labor Day. The men of your church get pumped up. They sign up in the lobby for the event several weeks in advance. Everyone is talking about last year when they roasted a whole pig on a spit. Gross and fascinating at the same time. The event comes and you have a great turnout. Everyone is excited about getting your new church year started right for the men.

And then . . . Well, I guess we better start getting ready for the Super Bowl Party in February. Then . . . the Spring Men's Weekend. Then . . . the Big Men's Rally again.

For this church, men's ministry is a series of "blips." Each year, there are three or four events that get guys excited. But in between, the church still struggles to get men to work in the nursery, the Sunday school classes have the same (old) people in them, and the monthly pancake breakfast is just about the only other men's activity available.

This is an event-driven men's ministry. Of course, events for men are important. We need lots of entry points for men to become involved in the life of the church and to get exposed to the gospel. But if the event is all there is, eventually men will stop coming.

You can escape the personality-driven men's ministry trap by continually recruiting and empowering leadership, which we covered in detail in chapter 7. Feel free to glance there now to review the strategies and suggestions for renewing your leadership.

How do you escape an event-driven men's ministry? Have a strategy in place to capture the momentum your events create and channel it into the right next step for every man.

Would you turn on the air conditioning in your house in the middle of the summer and then leave the doors and windows open? Of course not. In the same way, it takes a tremendous amount of work and energy to overcome inertia in men by creating value and momentum. Doesn't it make sense to have a concrete plan to capture that momentum and keep men moving forward in their relationship with God?

OVERCOMING A SKYSCRAPER MINISTRY

Imagine you are visiting New York City and a friend takes you to the top of a skyscraper. As you look over the beautiful city, he points to a building across the street and tells you about the wonderful restaurant on the top floor. "Why don't we just jump over there right now and have some lunch?"

You'd look across at the building, then down at the street, and conclude that your friend was crazy. It's ridiculous to think you could jump forty-five feet to another skyscraper.

Often the ministries and programs of our churches are like skyscrapers in New York City. Each of them exists without clear connection to other church programs. A person is involved in a Sunday school class and/or the praise team and/or a short-term mission trip, but there are no real connections between the initiatives. So getting a man who attends worship to join a couple's small group or a men's Bible study is like asking him to jump from one skyscraper to another.

The ironic thing is this: Some people are willing to make the jump. There are always the committed few who will take a leap of faith and dive headfirst into a new opportunity. In fact, enough people make these jumps in most churches to prevent us from seeing how poorly we have integrated a believable process of discipleship. But the vast majority of people will stay exactly where they are unless we build bridges to connect the opportunities together and make it obvious how to move from one step to the next. That's what it means to capture momentum.

Two Common Mistakes After Creating Momentum

There are two common mistakes that we tend to make after creating value with a man: We do too little, or we attempt to do too much.

First, we do too little. How many times have you seen a ministry expend all of its energy planning "the big event," only to pack up and go home after the closing "amen"? This is the classic event-driven men's ministry.

We hold a men's retreat or seminar; the man has a "blip." Next year we invite him . . . another "blip." The year after? "Blip" again. After a few years, we have a lot of "blippy" men, but there's no ongoing spiritual development.

If we are not careful, men will think this is what it means to be a good Christian. Or, they will lose interest because they don't see any lasting impact in their own lives. A roller coaster men's ministry builds a resistance in men to getting involved. Because they know, deep in their hearts, it's not really going to lead anywhere, your men (and your pastor) become inoculated against a viable discipleship process.

Second, attempting too much can be just as fruitless. For instance, you invite men to a big Super Bowl BBQ with lots of red meat and a giant screen TV. You encourage them to bring neighbors and friends, and several men who rarely darken the church's doors come. Then at halftime you get up and offer them an opportunity to join a forty-week study of the book of Revelation in the original Greek. A little over the top, but you see the point.

So how do you walk the line between these two extremes? Always have a right next step.

GIVE MEN A RIGHT NEXT STEP

When you plan an event or activity for men, make the follow-up opportunities part of your event planning. In other words, don't create momentum without a plan for how you will capture it (ever!). We'll cover each of the keys to successfully capturing momentum in detail, but for now, here's the list:
- Make the follow-up fit the event.
- Rightsize the commitment you are asking for.
- Always have an ending point.
- Choose good "second gear" material.
- Start new groups for new men.
- Help men take the next step—on the spot.

Make the Follow-up Fit the Event
As you plan an event, determine the types of men you will be targeting. You'll need to consider this as you plan the follow-up strategy too. The type of event you have will help determine what type of capture step to take. See Figure 12 for some ideas.

Type of Men	Type of Event	Follow-up Ideas
Men who need Christ	Super Bowl party	Softball team sign-up; adventure trip; new introductory small groups
Cultural Christians	Reroof a widow's house	Information meeting for mission trip; formation of servant ministry teams
Biblical Christians	Men's seminar or retreat	Small groups; class; service opportunity
Leaders	Lunch to discuss vision	Pray for men; attend a leaders' meeting as a guest

Figure 12

Rightsize the Commitment You Are Asking For

Don't ask men to overreach based on end-of-event enthusiasm. A man may initially be excited about the intense forty-week Bible study on godly manhood. But on Monday his customers start complaining, on Tuesday he remembers he's fifteen days late with his mortgage payment, and by Wednesday his enthusiasm has waned considerably.

You've driven a car and accidentally shifted from first to fourth gear. What happens? It's the same when we ask men to do too much too soon. They bog down. Most men on the fringe don't want to do a lot of preparation. Many men are not going to read a two-hundred-page book. So the event follow-up needs to scream to the man, "You can do this!!" It must be something he can actually visualize himself doing—with excitement. It has to be a "second gear" idea.

Always Have an Ending Point

We also can ask men to do too much by requiring open-ended commitments. Consider a man who has an experience that inspires him to seek a closer walk with God. He joins a weekly men's Bible study. Soon, either because his life circumstances change or perhaps because of overcommitment, his participation in the group starts to suffer. He misses a week here and there, then two weeks in a row, then three weeks. Finally, he just stops coming altogether. He leaves the group quietly, almost slinking away, feeling guilty that he let the group down, because there was no graceful exit strategy.

Now imagine the same man making a six-week commitment to meet with a group of men. If his circumstances change, he knows that he will only have to "tough it out" for a few more weeks to finish what he started. He leaves the group not in failure but with a sense of fulfillment and accomplishment. Which man will be more likely to join a small group at the next opportunity?

To reinforce this concept, you can even celebrate at the end of each cycle. This could be your time to share stories about how God has worked in your lives over the past six weeks, as well as say a formal good-bye to a man whose other commitments will not allow him to continue. Your group might even "commission" him for his new undertaking, making him feel like he is being sent by the group to the next thing, instead of feeling like he has abandoned them.

Choose Good "Second Gear" Material

Look for "cookies on the bottom shelf" materials that raise significant issues and deal with them biblically. Men will make a onetime, short-term commitment to something that seems "doable."

The case study in the box below illustrates two other common mistakes we often make. Can you find them?

MISTAKES IN MEN'S MINISTRY: A CASE STUDY

One church we'll call "Community Church" shared that they seemed to have reached a "ceiling" of sorts with the number of men who would engage in their small groups. When we asked them what they were doing to recruit men, their strategy seemed pretty sound, at first. They would have men's events in the church that had a broad appeal to the men. Every event was extremely well attended. At each event, they would offer an opportunity to join in a group for ongoing study. They were using good, second gear material. They were only asking for a short-term commitment. Everything seemed fine.

Then we asked the question: How are you signing guys up for the small groups? "Simple," they said. "We list all of the groups on a separate piece of paper in the back. Each group lists the name of the leader, when and where they are meeting, and how many spots they have available. So they find a group that's convenient and they write down their name, then the leader follows up.

"But only a few new guys ever sign up. And even those that do often don't show up."

Start New Groups for New Men

The first error Community Church made was listing groups with the number of spots available. A man who looks at that quickly realizes he is walking into an established group. Who else is in the group? How long have they been meeting? He is obviously going to be the "new guy." If you ever switched schools growing up, you remember what lunch was like for the first week. Everybody already had "their" table. You didn't really know how open they might be to a new kid sitting with them.

We might all be adults now, but that fear of rejection never goes away. Always start new groups for your follow-up.

Help Men Take the Next Step . . . on the Spot

Did you spot the second error? Don't have guys write their names on a list and tell them you'll "get back to them." You want men to leave feeling like they've already made the commitment. So whatever your next step, always ask for an on-site commitment.

Here's a proven method to get two-thirds of your men into follow-up small groups:

Hold an event that reaches a specific target group of men, like a seminar. Promote the event with—say it with us now—*personal invitations*. Before the event, recruit leaders who will commit to running a six-week follow-up group; have about one leader for every eight or nine men you expect to attend the seminar. (If two-thirds of the men sign up, that will give you groups of five or six for each leader.)

At the beginning or middle of the event, announce that there is a "next step" for everyone after the event. Show them the material they will be using, and make sure they understand that it is a short-term commitment. This gives them time to absorb the idea.

Brett often uses the following illustration during a seminar to explain the benefit of the follow-up groups:

"If you give me $100 now, I will give you $200 at the end of this seminar. How many of you would take me up on that offer?" Every hand usually goes up.

"Now, let me offer you a different deal. If you will give me $200 now, I will give you $1,000 in six weeks. Double the investment of the first deal, but five times the return. How many of you would take that deal?" Usually someone stands up and jokingly starts to take out his wallet at this point.

"Well, guys, this is exactly the deal I am offering you. If you will give me about eight hours of time over the next day at this event, I am going to give you a pretty good return on your investment. But if you will double that investment, and spend another eight hours over the next six weeks meeting with some other guys from this group to go over this study guide we're giving you, you will get five times as much out of it as if you just listened to me alone.

"The fact is that I can only give you information that will make you think during this seminar. If you really want to see how this will apply to your life, spend some time unpacking these issues with a few other guys who live in your world."

Provide several sessions for small-group discussion throughout the event. This helps model the follow-up groups and gets men talking to each other. We often hear of churches that had to break up the discussions to move to the next session.

About three quarters of the way through the event, instead of going into another small-group-discussion time, let your men know you will now be forming the groups for follow-up. Have each leader stand, introduce himself, and share when and where his group will be meeting. "Hi, I'm Don Smith. My group is going to meet at the Denny's on the corner of Fifth and Main on Thursday mornings at 6:30 a.m." And so on.

After all the leaders have introduced themselves, tell the men that for the next discussion time, you would like them to pick a group that they might be interested in continuing with after the event. Remind them it's only a six-week commitment. Tell them that even if they don't plan on attending a group afterward, just to go ahead and pick one for the discussion time.

At this point, all the men in the room are staring at you, and you have to say, "OK, right now! Pick someone to sit with! Get going!!!" They're men, remember? They will finally start moving, and before you know it each man will be sitting in a circle with some other men. It's messy, and looks unorganized, but it absolutely works! We guarantee it! The secret to this is that men are smart and will figure it out. You don't have to micromanage the process. In fact, micromanaging will actually reduce your effectiveness.

Before they get into the discussion, the leaders pass around a sheet of paper to collect each man's name, phone, and e-mail. Then they confirm the time and location of their very first meeting—make it within the next seven days—and adjust it if necessary to meet the men's needs. Then they briefly look at the material they will be using. (We provide a simple sixteen-page "Life Plan" with Man in the Mirror events.) If they have time, they'll go into the discussion questions for the session that just ended.

Even a man who might have gone reluctantly to sit in a group will become somewhat invested in when and where they will meet, what they will talk about, and who will be there.

Does it work? In events where churches use this method just the way it's described here, over two-thirds of the men indicate that they have decided to join the follow-up groups. Perhaps even more exciting, the percentage of men who have never been in a small group before and choose to be in the follow-up groups is even higher.

THE "NEXT STEP" MIND-SET

You can get everything else right, but if you consistently fail to capture momentum when you create it, you will not build a sustainable ministry.

In every interaction you have with a man, whether it is one-on-one over lunch, a small-group kickoff, a men's retreat or seminar, or any other activity, you should always be thinking, "What is a reasonable next step?" And then constantly communicate these steps to men.

Every leader in your ministry needs to have a capture momentum, "next step" mind-set. *Always show men a right next step.* Getting men to take a first step and then not showing them what's next is like leading a man to Christ and then abandoning him to live in the world with no discipleship. If you are not going to follow up, perhaps it would be better for Christ's kingdom to not raise men's expectations in the first place.

Will capturing momentum eliminate peaks and valleys in your ministry to men? No. You will still have men come and go, and you'll still have events or activities that draw lots of men who drop off. But over time your trend line will be sloping upward, indicating a sustainable ministry that continues to produce passionate disciples. (See Figure 13.)

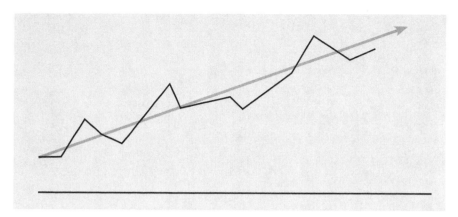

Figure 13
A Sustainable Men's Ministry
(General Upward Trend in Discipling Men)

One of the primary missions of the space shuttle is to put a satellite into space. The shuttle blasts into orbit, then an astronaut uses the robotic arm to pick up the satellite and place it in space, where it takes on the speed and trajectory of the shuttle itself. All according to plan.

Remember SkyLab? (All you under-forty-year-olds, check it out online at www.wikipedia.org.) The SkyLab was a huge satellite workstation—a precursor of the International Space Station. The United States put it into orbit in 1973, with plans of going up in the space shuttle in 1979 to boost it into a higher orbit. Unfortunately, the space shuttle wasn't ready until 1981. SkyLab didn't have enough momentum to hold its orbit that long, and it crashed to earth in late 1979. Luckily, the only casualty was an Australian cow.

> **THE BIG IDEA**
>
> Whenever you create momentum, always show men a right next step.

Be careful not to leave men in your church hanging. If you use an event to blast a man into a spiritual experience that draws him closer to God, don't just hope he can maintain his orbit. When a man crashes to the ground, there is always a lot more to worry about than an Australian cow.

So far, we have discussed how to build your ministry around a *vision*, how to *create* momentum with men, and now how to *capture* that momentum. In the next chapter we'll discuss how to *sustain* change in the men who have entered your discipleship process. We're only one step away from chapter 12, where we'll help you build a concrete plan to reach the men in your church.

Remember This

- Avoid a personality-driven men's ministry by constantly recruiting and renewing your leadership (see chapter 7).

- Escape an event-driven ministry by capturing the momentum your events create.

- Don't make men "leap" from one opportunity to the next. Build bridges that make it easy and intuitive for a man to move forward in his spiritual journey.

- Always give men a right next step.

- Remember these hints for your next step strategy:

    - Make the follow-up fit the event.

    - Rightsize the commitment you are asking for.

    - Always have an ending point. Choose good "second gear" material.

    - Start new groups for new men.

    - Help men take the next step—on the spot.

TALK ABOUT THIS

1. Do you feel like you have been on a roller coaster in your own spiritual journey? What seems to cause the peaks and valleys?

2. Does the roller coaster describe your men's ministry? If so, do you feel like you've fallen into the trap of an event-driven ministry? Personality-driven ministry? Both? What effect has this had on your energy and commitment to discipling men in your church?

3. List the events or activities you have done for men in your church over the last few months. Has there been a "capture" strategy in place for these events? If not, what could you have done to capture the momentum you created? If so, how could you have improved it?

4. What is the next event you have planned for men? Brainstorm with your team about how you will capture the momentum of this activity.

PRAY ABOUT THIS

Pray together with your leadership team . . .

• that God will give the men in your church a renewed desire to know Him.

• that your ministry will always provide a clear path for men to take from one opportunity to the next.

• that God continues to bond your leadership team together as a band of brothers focused on fulfilling the Great Commission among men.

SUSTAIN MOMENTUM THROUGH RELATIONSHIPS

From the event, to the next step, to . . . what? Once you get your men and your men's ministry off the roller coaster, how do you sustain spiritual progress? If you don't do anything, spiritual excitement will turn into little more than good intentions. One thing's for sure: Men won't make it on their own. But together, they can become authentic disciples who can change the world.

TO SUSTAIN MOMENTUM with men, get them into real relationships with other men who are seeking Christ. You can't sustain without small groups and one-on-one relationships. Why is this so important?

First, you want to help men *maintain the spiritual progress* they have made. This is particularly important for men early in their spiritual journey—those who need Christ and cultural Christians. Second, you want to get men into *regular prayer and the study of Scripture*. This is a particular focus for men who are biblical Christians and leaders, or who want to be. Building relationships will help you meet both of these objectives.

KEEPING CAPTURED GROUND

Military history is filled with stories about soldiers griping about surrendering ground they shed their blood to gain. "Take that hill!" they are told. "It is an integral part of our strategy!" And they do it, fighting valiantly to defeat the enemy and capture the ground—only to abandon it when the strategic winds shift in the command center. Pretty soon, the soldier loses confidence that there is any strategy at all. The cost is too high, the reward too fleeting.

Every effort you make that draws a man forward in his spiritual journey has a cost of its own: the time, energy, and focus of the leaders who planned and participated; and the opportunity cost to the man who chooses to participate in this activity instead of some other priority in his life. If you work hard to gain ground in the battle for men's time and attention but then don't find ways to sustain that effort, you'll just find yourself starting over. And the men themselves will begin to lose heart, feeling that nothing ever changes. As leaders, we must apply consistent effort, since progress in a man's spiritual journey is usually measured in small steps over a long period of time.

A LONG-TERM PERSPECTIVE

A ministry to men has to be more than just events; it must be about helping men to become mature in Christ. Again, it takes a long time to make a disciple. Almost always, discipleship takes place over a period of years in the context of significant relationships with other men.

We learned from our friend Chris White the importance of taking a "long-term, low-pressure" approach. There is no such thing as systematic, rapid spiritual growth. We must give men permission to stand around the rim of what we are doing and observe. Give them permission to buy in at their own pace, and let them come on board at their own level of involvement.

If you want to help other men grow in Christ, you will often feel that you want men to be successful more than they want it themselves. It would be easy for us to become impatient with new men who are not as mature as we might wish. Don't make men feel guilty because they are not becoming as "spiritual" as you want them to.

This is one of the biggest problems we see in men's ministry leaders—the leaders are frustrated, angry, and even bitter with their men because they are not as committed as the leaders would like. David was a speaker at a retreat one time when the leader of the men's mission trip stood up to make an announcement. "The mission trip is less than a month away and we only have four men signed up. I know in a church this large there are a lot of men who could go on this trip. Don't you know how fortunate you are? The people we are going to serve don't have anything. Frankly, I wonder whether some of you ought to seriously consider the level of your commitment to Christ."

After a few more minutes of his harangue, David felt like standing up in the back and saying, "Look, I'll go on the mission trip—as long as you stay home. As angry as you are I don't want to go anywhere for a week with you."

Men can sense your anger and frustration and they won't want any part of it. Our job is not to produce results—it's simply to be faithful.

SHOW MEN CHRIST VERSUS FIX THEIR BEHAVIOR

Too often we ask men to conform to our Christian men's subculture as a show of spirituality. "Use these buzzwords. Pray with this posture." When this happens, we can end up asking men to be "religious" at the expense of being spiritual.

Or, we ask them to perform certain activities to show their commitment to God. "If you love God, you will be in church on Wednesday night." One man readily responds to calls for "performance" Christianity because that's the nature of his relationship with his own dad, who has always made love conditional upon his son's performance.

It's ironic. The more we try to influence "behavior," the less real lasting change we see. Such an approach will simply burden men down and wear them out.

Q & A

What do you do when guys just don't "get it"?

You've been working to show Christ to a guy for months. But it seems like he goes out of his way to smoke and use foul language whenever your Christian friends come around. You know what? He's waiting to see if you'll be judgmental. Instead, love him. Get your friends in on the act. Surround him with godly men and he'll eventually decide he wants what you've got.

When men come to a prayer breakfast, conference, Bible study, or church, they come because they have an unmet need—a "void" to be filled. They come looking for a piece of bread they can drag away that will nourish their souls. They come thirsty for living water.

Rather than showing men a list of "dos" and "don'ts," we must show them Christ. Our job is not to "fix" their behavior. Our job is to make Christ ever more attractive so that He can do His life-transforming work in them. God's grace changes men, not some effort on their part to be good enough. When we help men connect with Jesus, He works the change in behavior from the inside out. He changes the desires of the man. We can only give a man a new rule book; Jesus will give him a new heart.

MEN WHO NEED CHRIST

Nowhere is this external focus more damaging than with men who need Christ. A man who has built up regular participation in one of your more accessible activities—like basketball or the softball team—is easily pushed away by someone telling him he's not behaving "correctly."

It is sometimes difficult for leaders to understand how to apply a "sustain" step to men early in their spiritual journey. After all, you can't really expect a man whose only experience with your church is participating in a sports outreach ministry to sign up for a twenty-four-week small group.

Sustaining change in a man who is just becoming aware of his need for Christ is much more about keeping "captured ground" than leapfrogging him to daily devotions and an accountability group.

For men at this stage, sustaining momentum may take place with opportunities very similar to the "create" step that got him involved in the first place. Remember, the key is relationships.

Consider the softball team as an example. One of your leaders, "Sam," has a neighbor named "Pete." After trading several favors, loaning each other tools and watching a playoff game together, Sam mentions he is on the church softball team. When Pete expresses interest, Sam invites him.

The season goes great. Everyone has a lot of fun on the team. No one takes it too seriously, though they all enjoy winning. Pete gets to know a few guys on the team. At the end of the season, they have a barbecue to celebrate, and the pastor comes to thank the guys for playing and representing the church with good sportsmanship.

The "create" step was the invitation to join the softball team. The "capture" step was the BBQ at the end of the year. Now what?

First, has Pete really progressed in his spiritual journey? Certainly! For ten weeks running he has spent an evening with a group of mostly Christian guys. They say a quick prayer before and after the game. Pete has begun to see that these guys are "normal." And there are some guys who have earned his respect.

Now you must find a way for Pete to maintain the relationships that he has begun to build. It may be another season of softball, or a weekly businessmen's luncheon that some of the guys go to. As these relationships begin to grow, Pete will have more opportunities to see Christ in these men's lives.

SUSTAIN BY CREATING A CULTURE OF PRAYER

One day, Bill, whose wife had just died of cancer, was talking with Pat, whose friend Tom Skinner was sick with leukemia. Pat said, "He's very sick. I guess the only thing we can do is pray."

Bill looked into Pat's face and said, "No, the thing we *can* do is pray."

We can't do anything without God's blessing, but we can do all things when we tap into the purpose of His will. Prayer is God's designated way to release His will in men's lives. Prayer is the currency of our personal relationship with Jesus. It will do us no good to leave it on account. We must take some out and spend it on men's souls. Prayer is the thing we can do.

Ensure that prayer is a part of everything you do for the men of your church. Train your leaders to integrate prayer into every activity. No man participating in an activity related to the church is going to be surprised by the inclusion of a prayer during the event.

Your leadership team ought also to be built on a foundation of prayer. But don't merely ask God to become a part of what you want to do in your church and city. Instead, pray that you will become a part of what God wants to do in your church and community.

HELP MEN DEVELOP A LOVE FOR GOD'S WORD

Disciples are "pupils." They are students of Jesus. They are men who desire to become more like Christ. To become like Him, they must first know Him.

We can say with confidence that we have never known a man whose life has changed in any significant way apart from the regular study of God's Word.

Some groups study Christian books (like those offered by Man in the Mirror, for which we are grateful), but book studies, fellowship groups, and prayer partner groups are no substitute for bringing men into direct contact with the living Lord through His living Word.

All men are affected by God's Word when they are exposed to it regularly. Have you noticed that when you are consistently in the Bible you begin to understand it better? Your desire for the Scriptures grows the more you interact with them. Unfortunately, the opposite is also true. When a man is not in the Scriptures very often, his desire for them doesn't have a chance to grow.

DEVELOPING DISCIPLE-MAKERS TO SUSTAIN YOUR MINISTRY

In his book *The Lost Art of Disciple Making,* Leroy Eims tells the story of a missionary named John, who spent the bulk of his years of service meeting with a few young men. Abruptly, his work was cut short when all missionaries were suddenly asked to leave the country.

THE **BIG** IDEA

We have never known a man whose life has changed in any significant way apart from the regular study of God's Word.

An observer who had once viewed John's ministry with skepticism years later marveled, "I look at what has come out of John's life. One of the men he worked with is now a professor mightily used of God to reach and train scores of university students. Another is leading a discipling team of about forty men and women. Another is in a nearby city with a group of thirty-five growing disciples. Three others have gone to other countries as missionaries. God is blessing their work."

Keep your eye out for men who want to make disciples. Obviously, you need to be involved with men at all levels. But can there be any doubt? The greatest return on your time will come from investing in a few "FAT" men—men who are *faithful, available,* and *teachable* (2 Timothy 2:2).

The focus of a men's ministry leader should be to make disciples of men who will in turn disciple others, and so on. This was the method of

Jesus. Your ministry to men will grow in proportion to your ability to build not just disciples but disciple-makers.

RECRUIT SHEPHERDS, NOT TEACHERS

Possibly the most important aspect of sustaining momentum is to make sure each of your men really feels like somebody cares about him. Look for leaders who are eager to show men the love of Christ, not their own biblical knowledge. Clark Cothern draws the distinction between two types of small-group leaders: one is a "question asker," the other, an "answer giver." One, a "group guide," the other, a "know-it-all narrator." One is a "dialogue traffic cop," the other, a "doctrine cop."[1] Men will respond best to leaders who help them find answers to questions without giving them the answer; guide men without showing off their knowledge; and help facilitate lively discussions, rather than show up men whose theology is still developing.

At a church of five thousand attenders in California, Wes Brown, the men's minister (yes, full-time), experienced a quantum leap in effectiveness when he changed his leadership model from "teaching" to "shepherding." In the beginning he recruited "teachers" to lead his small groups. Success was modest. After eleven years he had 137 men in small groups. Then he realized that what men really needed was someone who cared about them personally. He changed to a "shepherd" model and exploded to 750 men in just four years—a 550 percent increase!

LOVE YOUR WEAK MEN, DISCIPLE YOUR STRONG

Zechariah 11:15–16 explains the role of a shepherd further:

> Then the LORD said to me, "Go again and play the part of a worthless shepherd. This will illustrate how I will give this nation a shepherd who will not care for the sheep that are threatened by death, nor look after the young, nor heal the injured, nor feed the healthy." (NLT)

We can define the fourfold role of a good shepherd by looking at the opposite of the worthless shepherd in this passage:

- He cares for the sheep that are young.
- He cares for the injured.
- He cares for those threatened by death.
- He feeds the hungry.

This passage illustrates a basic rule for discipleship: *Love your weak men, and disciple the strong.* A good shepherd goes after those who are threatened by death. This might be men who don't know Christ, or men who are on their way to making major mistakes in their life. He creates a safe place where men with broken wings can heal—men injured by financial crisis, divorce, grief, addictions, or emotional issues. He takes care of the young, both spiritually and physically.

There will always be some men who constantly drain your emotional and spiritual energy. Good shepherds are committed to loving their weak men.

At the same time, God wants you to invest in faithful men who can disciple others. The faithful shepherd makes sure he feeds the healthy. How do you know when you should stop making an investment in a man who seems to not be going anywhere? It has to be a matter of prayerful consideration between you and God. Don't give up on any man—always be friendly, interested, and available—but there may come a time when God wants you to invest your time and energy in other men.

There are two errors leaders can make: to kick men out of the nest too soon, and to not challenge men to get out of the nest when it's time. "Disciple the strong" means men need to grow. If you don't help them, they will go to another church. We've all heard it said or said it ourselves: "I just didn't feel like I was being fed there." A good shepherd will "feed" the healthy.

In addition to feeding the healthy, a good shepherd propels strong men to take their next steps. He doesn't let men become complacent in their spiritual progress. Instead, he challenges them to step up to new opportunities, encourages them to go deeper in their faith, and urges them to serve others.

A PERSONAL INVESTMENT IN EVERY MAN

Your church already has many activities that men can be involved in. It doesn't have to be a "men's only" activity to help men grow spiritually. Remember the five groups of men in your church and community?

If you want to sustain momentum with each type of man, someone has to get to know each man in your church well enough to know where he is on his spiritual pilgrimage and what he needs to do to take the next step.

You have to develop enough leaders that they can take a personal interest in every man. Then you need to have ministry opportunities that will help men from each category move forward. This is where the hard work comes—there are no shortcuts here.

Men are good at keeping each other at a comfortable distance. It takes consistent time together to develop beyond the level of mere acquaintances.

We described these in detail earlier in the book, but here is a partial list of ways to engage men in relationships:

- Bible studies
- Ongoing ministry projects, such as mentoring teenagers
- Issue-oriented men's curriculum (family, marriage, work, etc.)
- Accountability groups
- Early morning leadership development with the pastor
- Prayer groups
- Issue-oriented support groups—divorce recovery, dealing with grief, etc.

Obviously, overlap will occur. Bible studies will pray. Book studies will address current issues as participants apply the Scriptures. Accountability groups will study books. The key is to engage men in ways that relate to where they live, work, and play.

Create a variety of opportunities for men to get better acquainted with Christ, since men will be motivated to know Him in many different ways. A restaurant with only one item on the menu will soon go out of business. The greater variety you offer, the more a man will find something that engages him where he walks.

SUSTAIN BY REACHING MEN'S HEADS, HEARTS, AND HANDS

In chapter 2, we introduced you to the concept that truth must be understood, believed, and lived out using the key words *head, heart,* and *hands.* This is an excellent paradigm to help you determine the "content" of your discipleship program. In other words, look at what you want men to know, believe, and do, and determine where in your church a man has the opportunity to learn, build his faith, and put it all into practice.

The University Presbyterian Church in Orlando used this paradigm to create a chart (see "What Does a Disciple Look Like?" below). Here's the key question: If you were to only have a man for five years, what would be the things you would want him to know, believe, and do in relation to four major areas of relationship—God, his family, the church, and the world—to feel like you had effectively discipled him?

For instance, you would want a man to know God's attributes and character, to believe that God loves him and died for him, and know how to pray and study the Bible. See the chart (Figure 14) for suggestions in all four relational spheres.

What Does a Disciple Look Like?

If you knew that you were only going to have a man for five years, what are the ideas and experiences that you would want him to get to consider yourself a "success"?

| ASPECT: | RELATIONAL SPHERE | | | |
	GOD	FAMILY	CHURCH	WORLD
HEAD (What do you know?)	Theology Scripture	Roles of husbands and fathers Family as covenant / significance in God's plan	Vision, Mission, Values Spiritual Gifts Ecclesiology	Missions Worldview
HANDS (What do you do?)	Worship Spiritual Disciplines	Communication Discipline Leadership Sacrifice	Ministry Stewardship Leadership Accountability	Vocation Missions Evangelism Social Justice Community
HEART (What do you love?)	Love God above self and all / no idols	Love family before self	Love church family before self	Love those who are desperate without Christ Love those who are suffering devastation from sin

Based on a chart developed by the leadership of University Presbyterian Church in Orlando, Florida.

Figure 14

You can take this chart and adapt it for your church's discipleship goals. Use it to audit your activities and events for men. Put an *X* beside each item that your church currently does well for men. This will help you identify potential holes or gaps where your "men's only" initiatives could have the biggest impact. Then you can plan to tackle areas that are not being addressed by other ministries of the church. A blank version is included at the end of the chapter to allow you to customize the chart for your church.

THE ARROWS ARE IMPORTANT TOO!

Sustaining momentum is the third "gear" in the engine that runs your conveyor belt. It is often the least exciting of the three parts of the Create–Capture–Sustain strategy. And yet it is here that the majority of spiritual growth takes place, and how you can best make sure no man is left behind.

Be sure to communicate to the leaders of your capture steps that their job is to help men make a seamless transition to your sustain activities. It's not enough to point men in the right direction and say, "Good luck!" We must have the mind-set that it is our responsibility to take men to the next step. Two previous examples of this are *personal invitations* (chapter 9) and *getting an on-site commitment* (chapter 10).

Consider this scenario: Your capture step after an activity is a six-week follow-up group; your sustain step is to get men and their spouses into a couple's class on Sundays at church. In the third or fourth week of the follow-up, the leaders begin introducing the idea of the men coming with their wives to the class on Sunday mornings.

At their last meeting, the leader might say something like this, "Guys, this has been a lot of fun. As I mentioned before, our next step is a couple's class on Sunday mornings. The teacher is John Thomas who does a great job. The next three weeks he's talking about divorce-proofing our marriages. My wife and I would like to invite you and your wives to meet us for the class and then come to our house for lunch after church. We'll meet you at the south doors to the education building at 9:10 this Sunday." Do you see how this is a concrete, believable opportunity that helps a man want to take the next step? Your leaders need to shepherd their men from one step to the next.

The arrows in the create–capture–sustain cycle are important! They represent a critical part of the system. We must develop seamless processes to move men along the continuum.

KEEP THE CONVEYOR BELT MOVING

The belt can't stand still; it needs to keep men moving forward in their spiritual journey. When they have gone through the cycle of create–capture–sustain, it will soon be time for another create opportunity. A twelve- or eighteen-week small-group study or Sunday school semester is great, but that sustaining activity needs to propel men forward to the next phase of their spiritual growth. Complacent men will get bored and eventually leave.

Incorporate the concept of resonance in your sustaining activities to help attract men to ongoing spiritual development opportunities. For instance, "Men's Sunday School Class" probably doesn't sound very interesting to most men. Simply calling your class "Winner's Circle for Men" or "Survival Training" ups the attention quotient. It says, "This is different than your preconception that all Sunday school classes are boring."

Finally, remember the portal priority. Make sure that all of the ongoing activities you are offering for men are helping them become disciples. Don't let them become places to stick men to keep them busy. Make sure all of your efforts are helping achieve the purpose of your men's ministry.

HAVING A LONG-TERM, SUSTAINABLE MEN'S MINISTRY

Perseverance and Patience Required

Manage your expectations and those of your leadership team. Don't expect more than the Bible promises. When you use the Vision–Create–Capture–Sustain strategy, expect men to drop away every time you ask for deeper levels of commitment. Why? Because the command to make disciples is juxtaposed against the principle of the parable of the sower. In other words, as you go along, some of the seed is snatched away, some withers, and some gets choked by life's riches and worries.

We should not expect a man to hear "the ten things every godly man believes" and completely "get it."

Some men will need several "cycles" of the create–capture before they're ready for the longer term spiritual growth of sustain. But by the end of each cycle you will also have new men staying involved in your discipleship process.

But don't expect less than the Bible promises either. (See John 3:16, 1 Timothy 1:15, Luke 19:10, Matthew 13:24, John 15:9, John 14:12.) *The problem is not that our plans are too big, but too small.* Raise expectations. Educate leadership (and yourself) about what's really going on. There is a spiritual battle raging for the souls of your men. The secular symptoms we see like crime, divorce, and workaholism are actually results of this spiritual war. God wants us to build Christ's kingdom.

Figure 15 shows the net effect on your ministry—long-term, sustainable growth. Notice the incremental increase in the number of disciples over time.

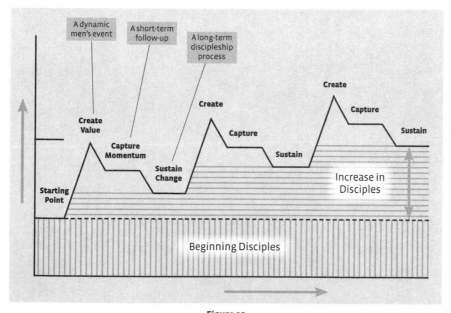

Figure 15
The Cumulative Impact of an Ongoing Strategy

173

Usually Not a Linear Process

Graphs such as Figure 15 make the process seem very neat and orderly. Create always leads to capture and then to sustain. In reality, though, these processes often overlap and intermingle. When a man is young in his spiritual journey, you have to keep creating compelling reasons for him to be involved in the discipleship process. *Remember, your ministry to men, and the paths men take toward spiritual maturity, will not be linear.*

The create step for one man may be the sustain step for someone else. For an unchurched guy, being on the softball team last season was a create step. He really enjoyed the end-of-season BBQ when he got to meet the pastor (a capture step). For him the next season of softball is a sustain step. For another man on the softball team, giving his testimony at the BBQ was a create step on his path to leadership. At the same time, one member of the team recruited another member to join his new small group (a capture step).

Sustaining momentum is the last step in the system. Now you have a complete picture of The No Man Left Behind Model. But understanding the concepts is not enough to actually make a difference in your church. So, in chapter 12 we will help you map out what it will look like in your church.

REMEMBER THIS

- Two goals for sustaining momentum in your ministry are to get men into relationships, and get men into small groups and the study of Scripture.

- It takes a long time to make a disciple. Don't get angry with men because you are more interested in their spiritual success than they are.

- Rather than showing men a list of "dos" and "don'ts," show them Christ.

- Build everything—your leadership team, your ministry, your discipleship programs, and every activity for men—on a foundation of prayer.

- We have never known a man whose life has changed in any significant way apart from the regular study of God's Word.

- Recruit shepherds—leaders who are eager to show men the love of Christ—not teachers—men who are eager to show men their biblical knowledge.

- Employ the concept of "resonance" in all of your sustaining activities. It's not a "Men's Sunday School Class," it's "Survival Training."

- Your ministry to men, and the paths men take through it toward spiritual maturity, will not be linear. The Vision–Create–Capture–Sustain strategy is a mind-set.

TALK ABOUT THIS

1. What activities help you sustain your own spiritual growth? What makes it effective? Great curriculum? Personal discipline? Other men accompanying you on the journey? What else? What are the implications for other men in your church?

2. What types of activities appeal the most to you? Ones that appeal to your intellect (head), your emotions and beliefs (heart), or that get you involved in something physical (hands)? Which of these does your church do the best? The worst?

3. Sometimes a *create* step can be a *sustain* step for someone else. Describe a situation like this in your own ministry.

4. Review the key points at the end of the chapter together and discuss the ones that you feel will have the most impact on your ministry.

5. As a team, use the chart on the next page to conduct an "audit" of your ministry offerings to men. Start by listing all the ideas and truths you want a man to have in each area. Put a checkmark next to each item that your church already provides for men. Circle any items that are not currently available.

PRAY ABOUT THIS

Pray together as a leadership team . . .

• that God will give you wisdom and patience as you seek to draw men closer to Him.

• that God would call men together into godly relationships where they will seek Him together.

• for men to become hungry for the Word of God.

• for strength for the journey as you make a long-term commitment to discipling men in your church.

WHAT SHOULD A DISCIPLE
LOOK LIKE IN YOUR CHURCH?

If you knew that you were only going to have a man for five years, what are the ideas and experiences that you would want him to get to consider yourself a "success"?

ASPECT:	RELATIONAL SPHERE			
	GOD	FAMILY	CHURCH	WORLD
HEAD (What do you know?)				
HANDS (What do you do?)				
HEART (What do you love?)				

Based on a chart developed by the leadership of University Presbyterian Church in Orlando, Florida.

BUILD YOUR PLAN:
HOW TO IMPLEMENT THE
MODEL IN YOUR CHURCH

YOU'VE MADE IT! Our goal was that by now you would be so full of ideas that you can't wait to get started. Hopefully, you already have.

Before you get too far, though, you might want to picture in your mind what success looks like. Is it a church full of men who are all involved in a small group? Is it the end of divorce in your church? Is it a church calendar full of activities that men can plug into no matter what their level of spiritual maturity?

"IT'S SO . . . NATURAL."

Imagine this: A man is being ordained or installed as an elder in your church. His family is standing on the stage with him. His wife is so proud of her husband—you can see it in her glowing face. Among those watching are a group of men who have made an impact on the man's life over the last several years, and men he has impacted as well.

The pastor steps up to him and says, "Tell us how God brought you to this point in your spiritual journey."

"To tell you the truth," he replies, "I'm not really sure. The only decision I can remember making is when my friend invited me to join the softball team six years ago. After that, it just seemed like every step I took was so . . . well . . . natural. Like I didn't have to decide what to do next. The right next step just always appeared when I was ready for it."

You've been to an airport with those long people movers. A guy steps on at one end, and off he goes. Sure, he can jump off the side or walk backward, but the system just naturally carries him forward toward the destination.

That's how a discipleship program for men in your church should work. A man makes a decision to step onto the belt, and off he goes. It has built-in momentum. And for the man, it's *natural*.

So What's Next for You?

Reading this book has been a *vision* and *create* step for you and your leadership team. The questions in the book and the exercises in this closing chapter will help you *capture* momentum. How well that momentum is sustained will be determined by the decisions you make by the end of this chapter, and the actions you take during the next twelve months.

So what comes next? Let's work our way back through the system and map out some next steps to implement The No Man Left Behind Model.

We start with the Napkin Test exercise. Use this to review the overall model. Then we focus on the eight components you'll need to build your plan. For each concept, a list of concrete steps or actions is provided to help you implement it in your ministry. We've split the activities into short-term—within the next three months—and longer-term—within the next year.

We don't want to micromanage you through this (because we want to model what we're asking you to do with your men). But neither do we want to leave you out in the cold. So here are a couple of ways you could complete your sustainable men's ministry plan.

Eight Sessions

Because this chapter gives you concrete next steps, you should not expect to complete it in one sitting or meeting of your leadership team. We suggest you take four sessions to work through the "Within the Next Three Months" activities and four sessions to work through the "Within the Next Year" activities.

If you are meeting with your team on a regular basis, spend your next four meetings on this chapter. (Have each man do the Napkin Test before your first meeting.) Each time, work through two components, completing the "Within the Next Three Months" exercises. After three to six months, have another series of four meetings to complete the "Within the Next Year" activities for each component. This will give you time to actually implement the plans you make.

Planning Retreat

You could also use a planning retreat for either or both of these sets of activities. Plan to have four sessions during the retreat and cover two of the components during each session. Usually it will be necessary to follow-up your retreat with a series of meetings to go over the implementation plans you draft.

During the next year, you will want to refer back to these plans to help you stay on course. As you do these exercises, record your work in a notebook or journal. This document will allow you to keep a record of your decisions, as well as facilitate sharing the information with your pastor and new leaders as they join your team.

We've included a handy checklist at the end to give you a sample schedule and to make it easy for you to see if you have completed all the exercises in the chapter.

Here we go . . .

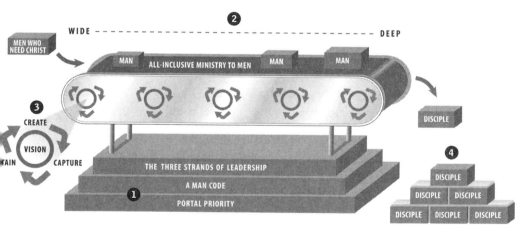

The No Man Left Behind Model
A System Designed to Produce Passionate Results

THE NAPKIN TEST

In the introduction, we explained we wanted to create a model that would pass "the napkin test." In other words, could you sit in a coffee shop and explain this model for men's ministry to another man with nothing but a napkin and a pen?

Looking at the illustration on the previous page, here is a quick synopsis of how to explain the model to another man:

1. Start with the three foundations of your ministry. Draw just the base on your napkin, showing three blocks: the *portal priority*, *man code*, and *three strands of leadership*. Briefly explain each one.

2. Then add the *continuum* and how it represents the spiritual journey toward becoming a disciple. Draw the conveyor belt with a couple of "man" bricks on it, showing the "wide-deep" continuum. Next, talk about how you're trying to get the men on a conveyor belt moving down this continuum, where every program and activity in the church is part of an *all-inclusive ministry to men* to help move men forward spiritually.

3. Now draw the engine for the conveyor belt: the *Vision–Create–Capture–Sustain* strategy. Draw the "vision" gear, showing the "Create–Capture–Sustain" components.

4. Finally, show them that the result of the model is men moving from wherever they start their spiritual journey to becoming *disciples* who help build the church. Be sure to draw the disciple "bricks" that come off the conveyor.

Within the next three months, take a friend to coffee or lunch, grab a napkin, and try it out! Use the space below to practice.

A PLAN FOR THE NEXT YEAR

1. Explaining the Portal Priority

The book began with your philosophy of ministry—discipleship is the portal priority. It is the lens that focuses all the church's different activities to achieve the outcomes you are seeking (see chapter 4). If you don't focus on disciple-making as your portal priority, you'll make donors, singers, and hard workers; not stewards, worshipers, or servants. In short, people will conform to the environment of the church and exhibit the correct behaviors, but their hearts will not change (Romans 12:2). External controls have no power to change a man's heart, but discipleship changes men from the inside out.

Here is a picture of the *portal priority.*

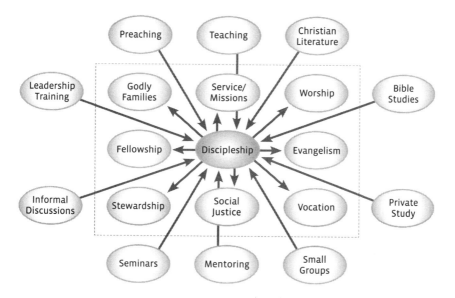

Make a new portal priority chart for your church. Revise the outcomes (inside the dotted line) as necessary to the outcomes your church is targeting. How does your church achieve these objectives? Revise the methods (outside the dotted line) and replace with the various activities available to the men in your church. Here's a three- to nine-month plan to do so.

Within the next three months:

❑ Identify two leaders who represent disciple-making efforts in your church; your small-groups pastor and a prominent Sunday school teacher, for example. Engage them in a discussion about the portal priority. Get their reaction to these methods to disciple men and women.

Within the next year:

❑Look for an opportunity to share the portal priority with all of the leaders of your church—perhaps on a leadership retreat, at a business meeting or staff meeting. You will, of course, need your pastor's buy-in first.

2. Modifying Your Man Code

Every man who walks into your church has an almost instant impression of how the church regards its men. From the decor to the bulletin to the quality of leadership, men quickly learn what it means to be a man in your church (see chapter 5). How can you help your church set the right man code for men?

Within the next three months:

❑ Look around your church for any obvious decorating that makes men feel welcome. Don't see any? Make some suggestions to the appropriate people about helping men feel more comfortable in your church. Start with your pastor and go from there. If you are able, offer to pay for the changes. Refer back to your work in chapter 5 and list some changes you would suggest.

Within the next year:

❑Get a group of men together to discuss making the environment of your church more friendly to men. Record a few ideas below and pick the best one(s) to implement. Here are a few samples to get you going:

- Create a men's section for your bulletin. Don't fill it with boring announcements. Have different men write a short testimony for the bulletin once a month. Make it sound challenging and fun to be a man in your church.
- Redo the men's restroom. Put a bulletin board over every urinal and post your "external challenge" to men, announcements about the men's ministry, along with jokes and the sports page.

What other ideas do you have?

_____

_____

_____

_____

_____

3. Developing the Three Strands of Leadership

The cord of three strands is not easily broken. The three strands of leadership for your ministry to men are: your senior pastor, a passionate leader, and a committed leadership team. (For a detailed discussion, review chapter 6.) *Within the next three months:*

❑ Pray for your pastor regularly, both individually and with other leaders. Get into the habit of including your pastor in all communications about the men's ministry. Discuss with your leadership team ways you could become known as the pastor's ardent supporters. Write down some specific ways you and your leadership team could be an encouragement to the pastor. (Start here or use a notebook or journal to record your responses.)

_____

_____

_____

_____

❑ Do you have a passionate leader for your ministry to men? If so, write down his name here (or in your notebook or journal). If not, write down the names of several men who are possibilities. Begin to pray that God would raise up His man.

_____

_____

_____

_____

❑ Use the two columns on the next page (or make them in your notebook/journal). In the first, list the members of your ministry leadership team here. Do they represent the five types of men in your church whom you are trying to reach? If not, list men in the second column whom you might possibly recruit to your leadership team. Within the next three months, get with one of these men and share your vision for discipling men.

MEN ON THE MINISTRY TEAM   CANDIDATES FOR THE MINISTRY TEAM

_____   _____

_____   _____

_____   _____

_____   _____

Within the next year:

❑ Plan a major act of appreciation for your pastor. Have a men's or couples banquet with your pastor as the surprise guest of honor; arrange for their lawn to be cared for during the entire summer; or find a cabin the pastor and spouse can escape to for a week away from it all. Write down some ideas and pick one or two to pursue.

_____

_____

_____

_____

❑ Do you need to recruit more men for your leadership team? Meet with a different potential leader over coffee or lunch every month for a year. Make it a habit to always be looking for the next man with whom you can share your vision. Get with your leadership team to make a list of men whose active involvement you will seek.

_____

_____

_____

_____

❑ Your leadership team must become to each other what they hope the men of the church will become. Select a discipleship curriculum of some type for your leadership team to go through together. There are lots of materials available from your denomination, Man in the Mirror, or other organizations such as The Navigators, Men's Fraternity, or Top Gun.

4. Developing an All-Inclusive Ministry to Men

Everything your church does that touches men is men's ministry, even if it's not a men's only program. Your men's ministry is made up of every man in your church, plus the men you'd like to be there. (For a detailed discussion, review chapter 7.) Look for opportunities for the men's ministry to support the other ministries of the church. Also, look for ways to connect more men to the different initiatives that are working to disciple men in your church.

Within the next three months:

❏List some existing ministries in your church not traditionally considered "men's ministries." What are concrete ways you could help them reach men more effectively?

_____

_____

_____

_____

Within the next year:

❏Help every man in your church come to the realization that he is part of your men's ministry. How could you achieve that? List eight or ten major ways that men are involved in your church, and beside each one write down one or two concrete steps to help them feel a part of what God is doing through the men of your church.

Example:

Men working in the nursery.

Give them smocks with the men's ministry logo.

Men helping in youth sports league.

Have an appreciation banquet for coaches / referees.

_____

_____

_____

_____

_____

_____

_____

_____

5. Clarifying Your Vision

Help men answer the question, "Why are we doing this?" Everyone wants to feel like they're making a contribution, like they're achieving something. A ministry that is just a series of disconnected activities will soon run out of steam.

In chapter 8 you worked on an internal purpose statement, an external call, and an elevator speech. Having a clear vision helps you focus your energy to achieve worthy goals:

- Your *internal purpose statement* helps your leadership team decide what you will and won't do.
- Your *external slogan* needs to resonate with men, calling them to be a part of something bigger than themselves.
- The *elevator speech* explains your vision for men in a few short sentences, and is particularly helpful in recruiting new leaders.

Within the next three months:
❑ Develop an external call for your men's ministry efforts. Write down some ideas here (or in your notebook or journal), and work on it as a team. Get the acceptance and support of your pastor(s) and other leaders.

_____

_____

_____

_____

Within the next year:
❑Develop a new internal purpose statement for your men's ministry. Don't forget, your purpose statement is dynamic. It can change from year to year as your objectives change. But make sure your purpose statement is in keeping with the mission of the church.

Refer to the work you did in chapter 8 and write a draft statement below. Get more men involved in reviewing and agreeing to these priorities.

_____

_____

_____

_____

_____

_____

❑ Help each man in your leadership team develop an elevator speech —three to five sentences that explain your vision for the men of the church. You could start with your draft from chapter 8 and get feedback from other men. Then distribute your final draft to other leaders and ask them to personalize the speech for their own use with men.

6. Creating Value

We create momentum by attracting men to go to the next level. We do this by providing something of value to them. For guys at the beginning of their journey, it may be fun and fellowship. But as a man moves forward, he needs to have his spiritual needs met more directly.

Note: For the _create_ and _capture_ exercises below, be sure to refer back to the work you did in the "Talk About This" discussion questions at the end of chapters 9 and 10.

Within the next three months:

❑ Do you have any events planned in the near future? Write them down below. Then indicate which of the five types of men each event will focus on, and how you will personally invite men to attend. What might you change about these events based on what you have read?

_____

_____

_____

_____

_____

_____

_____

_____

Within the next year:

❑ Use separate paper or a spreadsheet to plan out a twelve-month calendar for _create_ opportunities for the men of your church. (Remember these do not have to be men's only initiatives, and, as we've said elsewhere, they don't even have to be planned by your leadership team.) Try and make sure there is at least one opportunity for each of type of man in your church during the year. Also, make sure that your activities support the men's ministry's overall purpose.

7. Capturing Momentum

There's no point in giving men some kind of emotional or spiritual high without giving them the right next step they need to maintain the ground they've gained. Never create momentum—whether it's a big event or lunch with a new man—without a plan for what's next. Adopt the "right next step" mind-set to avoid wasted efforts. The right next step is always concrete and achievable—a man leaves already having made the commitment and knowing what he will do next.

Within the next three months:

❏ Look at the events and opportunities you already have scheduled for men. Does each activity have a clear and appropriate next step for the men who participate? Refer to your list above and write down what the next step will be for each activity or event occurring in the next six months. Begin to build a chart that shows "pathways" through your men's discipleship programs. See the examples below and use the chart at the end of the chapter.

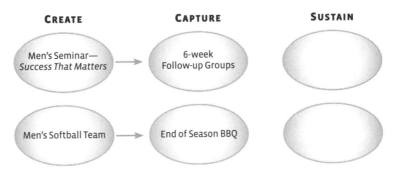

Note: It is possible to have more than one *capture* opportunity for a *create* activity. For instance, if you are creating momentum for a leader by having coffee with him to discuss your vision for discipling men, you may invite him to pray for some specific needs and how he might want to get involved, invite him to your next leadership team meeting, or, based on his interest, invite him to a small-group leaders training class. Any of those would be suitable *capture* steps.

Within the next year:

❑ Adopt the right next step mind-set in all of your interactions with men. Now that you've learned this technique of charting your activities, every time you plan an activity of any type, draw a "pathway" for a man who attends that shows what the *capture* step(s) will be. Assign each activity to a leader who will ensure that these follow-up steps are actually executed.

8. Sustaining Momentum

Long-term change almost always happens in the context of relationships. How will you engage men in relationship-based discipleship opportunities in the church? *Sustain* change in men's lives by focusing on their heart, not their behavior. (Review chapter 11.) Don't allow men to look good on the outside but be hollow and dead on the inside. Challenge men's motivations more than their behavior.

Within the next three months:

❑ Make a list of all of the different ongoing discipleship opportunities in your church according to the five types of men described in chapter 11. For example, include Sunday school classes, small groups, and service opportunities.

MEN WHO NEED CHRIST

_____

_____

_____

_____

MEN WHO ARE CULTURAL CHRISTIANS

_____

_____

_____

_____

MEN WHO ARE BIBLICAL CHRISTIANS

_____

_____

_____

_____

MEN WHO ARE LEADERS

_____

_____

_____

_____

MEN WHO ARE HURTING

_____

_____

_____

_____

❑ How will you plug men into these activities? Use the chart at the end of the chapter to map how you will connect men at the *capture* step to the ongoing discipleship opportunities listed above. Here's an example of a "completed" pathway:

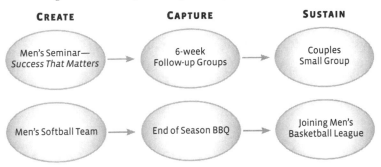

CREATE	CAPTURE	SUSTAIN
Men's Seminar—*Success That Matters* →	6-week Follow-up Groups →	Couples Small Group
Men's Softball Team →	End of Season BBQ →	Joining Men's Basketball League

Note: There can also be multiple *sustain* opportunities after a *capture* step. For instance, you may offer the men in the six-week follow-up groups a choice between staying in their groups for another six or twelve weeks, joining a couples small group with their wife, or joining a regular Sunday school class. Remember that the leader of the *capture* step is personally responsible for shepherding men into the *sustain* activity.

Within the next year:

❑ Refer back to your head-heart-hands chart from chapter 11. Do you see any holes in the current offerings of the church for men? Plan to develop new longer-term discipleship opportunities for men that fill these gaps. These will need to be implemented over the next several years. Make a list below of two or three different *sustain* opportunities not currently available that you would like to offer men. Begin praying about the steps you will need to take to make these a reality.

_____

_____

_____

Don't forget to keep repeating the cycle with men. That is the key to keeping men moving down the continuum.

YOUR CHECKLIST OF SHORT- AND LONG-TERM ACTIVITIES

Here's a checklist of the short- and long-term activities compiled from above.

Within the Next Three Months

Session One:

❑ Do the napkin test with a friend.

❑ Discuss the portal priority with two disciple-making leaders in your church; for instance, the small-groups pastor and a Sunday school teacher.

❑ Compile a list of subtle decorating changes that would make your church more welcoming to men. Discuss it with your pastor.

Session Two:

❑ Make it a habit to pray for your pastor regularly both individually and with leaders.

❑ Make a list of specific ways you could be an encouragement to the pastor.

❑ If you don't have an overall men's ministry leader, make a list of men passionate about discipleship and pray that God will call His man to lead your ministry.

❑ Make a list of men on your leadership team. Make a second list of men you might want to recruit to your team to help you reach the five types of men described in chapter 11.

❑ Make a list of existing ministries in your church not traditionally considered men's ministries. Look for concrete ways to help them reach men more effectively.

Session Three:

❏ Develop an external call for your men's ministry efforts.

❏ For any upcoming *create* events, determine which of the five types of men the event will target, and how men will be personally invited to the event.

Session Four:

❏ Determine the *capture* step(s) for each *create* event you listed, and begin a chart that shows "pathways" men will follow.

❏ Make a list of all the different ongoing discipleship opportunities of your church, organized according to the five types of men (*sustain*).

❏ For each *create–capture* pathway, chart the potential *sustain* step(s) that a man could take at the end of the *capture* step.

Within the Next Year

Session One:

❏ Share the portal priority with all of the leaders of your church.

❏ Gather a group of men to discuss making your church environment more friendly to men, from the decor to the bulletin to the worship. Start implementing a few ideas.

Session Two:

❏ Plan a major act of appreciation for your pastor. Be creative.

❏ Share your vision for discipling men with a different potential leader every month. Get members of your leadership team to commit to doing this as well.

❏ Start a discipleship curriculum with your leadership team.

❏ Make a list of ways men are involved in your church. Design a concrete step to make those men feel involved in what God is doing through the men of your church.

Session Three:

❏ Develop a new internal purpose statement.

❏ Help each man on the leadership team develop his elevator speech.

❏ Create a twelve-month calendar for *create* opportunities. Start with activities already planned by your church that men can participate in, then add men's only events to ensure that all five types of men will be reached at least once.

Session Four:

❑ Determine the *capture* step for every *create* opportunity in your calendar—even those that are not men only. Chart the *create–capture* sequences to build pathways men will follow.

❑ For each *create–capture* pathway, chart the potential *sustain* step(s) that a man could take at the end of the *capture* step.

❑ Using the head-heart-hands chart, look for "gaps" in your church's current ongoing discipleship opportunities for men. Make long-term plans to develop *sustain*-type opportunities to fill those gaps.

Use the chart below (or make your own) to map out "pathways" for men through your discipleship programs.

PATHWAYS THROUGH DISCIPLESHIP

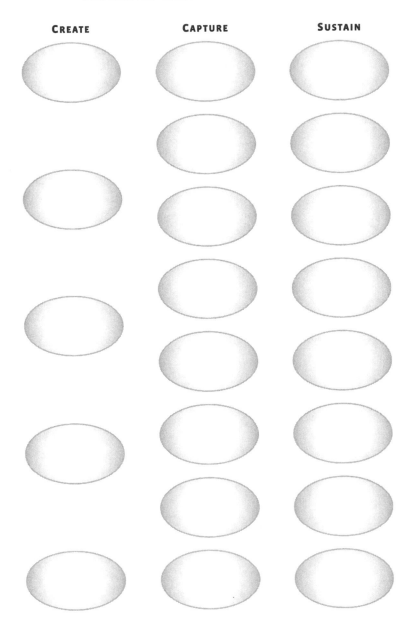

EPILOGUE:

RAISING UP
FOURTH SEED LEADERS

WOULD YOU LIKE to be a Fourth Seed Leader?

In the parable of the sower, Jesus described four seeds. Of the fourth seed He said, "But the one who received the seed that fell on good soil is the man who hears the word and understands it. He produces a crop, yielding a hundred, sixty or thirty times what was sown" (Matthew 13:23).

A Fourth Seed Leader is a person who "gets" the gospel, increasingly feels humbled by the grace of God, and lives in the overflow of a vibrant relationship with Jesus. Fourth Seed Leaders feel like they will explode unless they can lead others to Christ and help them grow.

Fourth Seed Leaders must share the gospel or they cannot be happy. They want to "bear much fruit, showing [themselves] to be [Christ's] disciples" (John 15:8). How much fruit? It may be one hundred, sixty, or thirty times what was sown.

WHERE ARE THE FOURTH SEED LEADERS?

As we mentioned earlier, in the United States there are 350,000 churches (with an average attendance of about one hundred people) and 108 million men age fifteen and older. We estimate that 1 percent of all American men are Fourth Seed Leaders—leaders passionate about reaching men for Jesus Christ. That would be about one million men—roughly three per church. Many women also are passionate about seeing men find faith.

NEEDED: MORE FOURTH SEED LEADERS

Some leaders are content reaching a circle of three, six, or even ten people. Let's applaud this—better six souls than the zero that many Christians reproduce. But to achieve Christ's vision to make disciples of every willing man, woman, and child, we also need leaders who *dream big, think big, risk big*. Are you a leader who wants to reach your entire church, your whole city, all your peers? Are you a leader who wants to reach thirty, sixty, one hundred or more souls for Jesus Christ? Are you committed to the vision that no man will be left behind? Would you like to see God do something great through your life? If so, welcome to the battle for men's souls—you are a Fourth Seed Leader.

Our prayer is that this book has equipped you to implement a discipleship system in your church and reproduce yourself like the fourth seed in Jesus' parable. We pray it also helps you raise up other leaders to join you.

WHY "NO MAN LEFT BEHIND"?

God has given us the responsibility and privilege of spiritual leadership. He has called us to disciple every man in our churches and communities. The consequences are too important for us not to do our absolute best to be faithful.

Above all else, leadership is a calling—a calling from God. Your life and ministry can be a spiritual outpost for men—a rescue mission, a halfway house, a hospital for men with broken wings. We are here to help men change the core affections of their hearts, to help them believe that the gospel can change their lives, to show them a living (though imperfect) example of a man or woman after God.

Jesus entrusts men to us. Jesus said, "After a long time the master of those servants returned and settled accounts with them. The man who had received the five talents brought the other five. 'Master,' he said, 'you entrusted me with five talents. See, I have gained five more.' His master replied, 'Well done, good and faithful servant! You have been faithful with a few things; I will put you in charge of many things. Come and share your master's happiness!'" (Matthew 25:19–21). We are not responsible for the outcomes with our men, but we are responsible to be faithful to them.

Responsibility requires commitment. "Not many of you should presume to be teachers, my brothers, because you know that we who teach will be judged more strictly" (James 3:1). We remind ourselves that the stakes are high.

This also requires a team effort. If you read this book by yourself, begin to pray about other men whom God might call to join you in your efforts to disciple men. As you will see, no leader can do this on his own.

To lead men is also a rare and holy privilege. We get to join God Himself in His work. All around us a battle rages for men's souls. God is with us in the battle; together we can win. We cannot, we must not, and by God's grace, we will not fail!

Therefore, let us pledge to be found faithful.

God, we pray for the strength, wisdom, and time to produce a crop—one hundred, sixty, or thirty times what You have sown into us. Help us to faithfully discharge the responsibilities of discipling men to which we now pledge ourselves. And may You use this book in the lives of leaders to ensure that no man is left behind. In the powerful name of Jesus, amen.

Are you a Fourth Seed Leader? Would you like to connect with other leaders like you for encouragement, to share ideas, and learn best practices? Send an e-mail to fourthseedleader@maninthemirror.org for information about how to join the Leadership Community. You'll get access to special online resources and be on the leading edge of the men's discipleship movement.

THE BIG IDEAS

We've collected the Big Ideas from each chapter into one page to help you review the major concepts of The No Man Left Behind Model. (This should help you pass the napkin test!)

1. The discipleship system of your church is perfectly designed to produce the kind of men you have sitting in the pews.

2. A spiritual reformation of society starts with a spiritual reformation of men.

3. A disciple is called to walk with Christ, equipped to live like Christ, and sent to work for Christ. (*Disciple*)

4. Christianity is not about behavior modification; it's about heart transformation.

5. Within a few weeks, a man understands what it means to be a man in your church. (*Man Code*)

6. The three strands of leadership for your ministry are the senior pastor, a primary leader, and a leadership team. (*The Three Strands of Leadership*)

7. Build a seamless process to move men across the wide-deep continuum.

8. An all-inclusive men's ministry maximizes the kingdom impact of every interaction with every man, no matter the setting. *(An All-Inclusive Ministry to Men)*

9. Ideas are more powerful than labor. Ideas set forces in motion that, once released, can no longer be contained. *(Vision)*

10. Give men what they need in the context of what they want. *(Create)*

11. Whenever you create momentum, always show men a right next step. *(Capture)*

12. We have never known a man whose life has changed in any significant way apart from the regular study of God's Word. *(Sustain)*

NOTES

Chapter 1: Men's Ministry Is Rocket Science

1. Richard Foster, *Celebration of Discipline*, 25th anniv. ed. (New York: Harper Collins, 1988), 107.
2. "Most Adults Feel Accepted by God, but Lack a Biblical Worldview," *The Barna Update*, August 9, 2005, available at www.barna.org.
3. *Yearbook of American and Canadian Churches* (Nashville: Abingdon, 2003), 386.
4. U.S. Census Bureau; Wade F. Horn and Tom Sylvester, *Father Facts*, 4th ed. (Gaithersburg, MD: National Fatherhood Initiative, 2002).

Chapter 2: No Man Fails on Purpose

1. American Academy of Pediatrics, "Family Pediatrics Report of the Task Force on the Family," 2003, *Pediatrics* 111(6): 1541–71.
2. James Dobson, *Bringing Up Boys* (Wheaton: Tyndale, 2001), 160.
3. "Swim with the Sharks (and Survive)," *Go!* Magazine, a publication of North American Mission Board, [electronic version]. http://www.go.studentz.com/my_life/swim_with_the_sharks.htm, retrieved 12 February 2004.
4. Ralph Mattson and Arthur Miller, *Finding a Job You Can Love* (Nashville: Thomas Nelson, 1982), 123.
5. Howard Dayton, president of Crown Financial Ministries, personal correspondence, January 2004.
6. Family Safe Media, retrieved 12 February 2004 from http://www.familysafemedia.com/pornography_statistics.html.
7. American Academy of Pediatrics, "Family Pediatrics Report," 1541–71.
8. "Most Adults Feel Accepted by God but Lack a Biblical Worldview," *The Barna Update*, 9 August 2005; available at www.barna.org.
9. Population statistics: No 14, "Resident Population Projections by Sex and Age: 2000 to 2050, U. S. Census Bureau," "National Population Projections—Summary Tables"; published 13 January 2000; retrieved February 2003 from www.census.gov/population/www/projections/natsum-T3.html. In 2005 men age fifteen and older were 110,545,000. We use fifteen for manhood because this is the age when young men tend to get a job and the car keys. Earning

money and driving a 2,000 pound vehicle is as good a way as any to
determine "adulthood."

10. Estimate based on 39 percent indicating they are "born again";
retrieved from Barna Group at http://www.barna.org/cgi-bin/
PageCategory.asp?CategoryID=19.

11. According to the Barna Group (2000), of the 16 percent of churched
adults involved in discipleship, 69 percent rely upon small groups for
their growth, and one-fifth (20 percent) rely upon Sunday school (11
percent on other classes) to grow spiritually; www.barna.org/Flex-
Page.aspx?Page= BarnaUpdate&BarnaUpdateID=61.
The following two stats do not take into consideration how participation in discipleship may vary by gender:
- 16 percent of America's 38,880,000 men who attend church in
  discipleship = 6,000,000
- 69 percent of 6,000,000 in small groups = 3,500,000

12. "U.S. Congregational Life Survey: What Are the Major Challenges
That U.S. Congregations Face?" 26 October 2002, www.uscongrega
tions.org/key.htm#congregations.

Chapter 3: What Is a Disciple?
1. Richard Baxter, *The Refined Pastor*, ch. 2, sec. 1, 4.4.

Chapter 8: Vision: A Compelling Reason for Men to Get Involved
1. N. W. Saunders, trans., *Greek Political Oratory* (New York: Penguin,
1970). Pat and David recounted the story of Demosthenes and
Isocrates previously in their book *The Dad in the Mirror* (Grand
Rapids: Zondervan, 2003).

Chapter 9: Creating Momentum by Providing Value
1. Francis Schaeffer, *Escape from Reason* (Downers Grove, IL:
InterVarsity, 1968), 94.

Chapter 11: Sustain Momentum through Relationships
1. *Discipleship Journal's 101 Best Small-Group Ideas*, Deena Davis, comp.
(Colorado Springs: NavPress, 1996), 22–23.

APPENDIX A

Twenty-Five Ways to Connect
with Your Pastor

If we want to connect with our pastors, the overarching idea is don't put demands on them. Instead, help them accomplish their mission. In that way, we become a part of their ministry instead of the object of their ministry. Here are twenty-five additional ideas:

DO

1. Write your pastor a note affirming a job well done. Think of something very specific they do well (e.g., what they say when they baptize someone).
2. Invite your neighbors to church and introduce them to your pastor after the service.
3. Tell your pastor you are praying for them—and then do it. If you are close enough, ask for specific prayer requests.
4. Always speak well of your pastor. Little birds inevitably chirp when you say bad things.
5. Always defend your pastor. The principle is, "I stick up for my friends."
6. Ask your pastor what their goals are and how you can help them.
7. Volunteer to serve in the church.
8. Offer to babysit so your pastor and spouse can go out on a date.
9. Pick their favorite restaurant and present a gift certificate for the pastor and their spouse to go out alone.
10. Volunteer to start a small group to disciple some of the men in the church—better yet, just do it.
11. Ask for their opinion about what discipleship materials you should use.
12. Make sure they receive a good salary and have a funded retirement plan.
13. Be a balanced and godly man, husband, and father yourself. Be a blessing rather than a burden to your pastor.
14. Tithe.
15. Be in a small group.
16. Pray with your wife. (This will reduce your pastor's counseling load.)

17. Read your Bible every day. Fill up with the Word of God, and it can't help but overflow in ways visible to others but probably not to you.
18. Take your children to Sunday school. Godly children are a blessing in any church.

DON'T

19. Don't ask your pastor to lunch to share your love and appreciation. Just say it—or better yet, send a handwritten note. Respect the fact that time is their most limited resource.
20. Don't offer constructive criticism until you have earned the right (ten praises before you even come close to qualifying for one constructive comment).
21. Don't criticize your pastor behind their back. If you like what's going on, tell your friends. If you don't like what's going on, tell your pastor (but refer to previous "don't").
22. Don't expect him to be Chuck Swindoll, Bill Hybels, or Andy Stanley.
23. Don't put pressure on them to put resources into your program. Instead, just start discipling men and, as your ministry grows, tell or send your pastor success stories. Results first, then support follows in its proper order.
24. Don't be angry with them for only being human.
25. Don't put pressure on them that will strain their health, marriage, children, or finances.

Adapted from *The Weekly Briefing*, by Patrick Morley, volume 126. Available online at www.maninthemirror.org.

APPENDIX B

Sample Vision Statements

The following vision components—internal purpose statements, external slogans, and ministry names—were submitted by various churches with whom Man in the Mirror has worked. We appreciate their willingness to share them.

Internal Purpose Statements

1. The purpose of Iron Man Men's Ministry is to help the men of our church become disciples—men who are called to walk with Christ, equipped to live like Christ, and sent to work for Christ (2 Timothy 3:15–17).

   We will do this by helping men develop authentic relationships with Christian men that will help them:
   - Find the true meaning of the gospel through relevant teaching and shared experiences,
   - Become leaders in their households and in the church, and
   - Be living examples of the gospel in the marketplace, the community, and the world.

2. [Our purpose is] Developing godly men and leaders, through training on the practical, day-to-day applications of the Word of God and through service to meet the various needs of the community.

3. Growing godly men through relational discipleship and the power of the Holy Spirit.

4. To build relationships with men, to encourage them practically, and bring them closer to Christ through fellowship, mentoring, and discipling.

5. To become a community of transformed men who leave a lasting legacy to the honor of Jesus Christ.

6. To encourage and equip every man to be committed, competent, creative, and compassionate in serving others for the glory of God.

7. The purpose of our men's ministry is to . . .

- help connect men into deeper relationships with other Christian men who encourage, support, and pray for each other in their struggles against all types of sin. "As iron sharpens iron, so one man sharpens another" (Proverbs 27:17).
- help men start or continue their journey toward becoming an authentic Christian man who follows Jesus. "Therefore go and make disciples of all nations, baptizing them in the name of the Father and of the Son and of the Holy Spirit" (Matthew 28:19).
- equip men for spiritual service in the home, workplace, and community while finding proper balance for their commitments to family, work, and faith. "If they obey and serve him, they will spend the rest of their days in prosperity and their years in contentment" (Job 36:11).

External Slogans

Sharpening Men to Transform the World
Brothers in the Great Adventure
Training Men for the Battle
First In . . . Last Out . . . No Man Left Behind
Changing Men's Hearts One at a Time
His Work in Progress
Transforming Our Community, One Man at a Time
ADAPT (Accountability, Discipleship, and Prayer Together)
Preparing Men—Proclaiming Christ

Ministry Names

Iron Men (or Iron Man)
Band of Brothers
Fishers of Men
Men of A.I.M. (Action, Integrity, Maturity)
FirstPursuit
Men of Adventure
Journeymen

APPENDIX C

Creating Momentum for the Five Types of Men
(Forty ideas across the Continuum)

WIDE			DEEP	
Type 1: **NEED CHRIST**	Type 2: **CULTURAL CHRISTIANS**	Type 3: **BIBLICAL CHRISTIANS**	Type 4: **LEADERS**	Type 5: **HURTING MEN**
Softball team	Men's seminar—like Success That Matters	Small group	Officer training	Grief recovery groups
Basketball league	Financial seminar	Bible study	Small-group leaders workshop	Crown financial seminar
Hunting/fishing outing	Church picnic	Men's retreat	Accountability group	Parenting-a-difficult-child class
Adventure trip (1-day)	Service project	Sunday school class	Christian Leadership Concepts (two-year intense curriculum)	Divorce recovery group
Classic car club	Adventure retreat	Mission trip	Leadership training	Sexual-addictions group/counseling
Car Care Day for single moms	Men's BBQ	Ongoing service opportunity (like a homeless shelter)	Off-site conferences and leadership seminars	Marriage counseling
Daddy-daughter dance	Promise Keepers rally	Rite of passage for youth (reaches their parents too) like *A Chosen Generation*		Curriculum from Pure Life Ministries
Sporting events	*Authentic Manhood* from Men's Fraternity	*Basic Training* from Top Gun		
Paintball		Promise Keepers rally		
Job fair				

NOTE: Remember that the fifth type, men who are hurting, can be found in each of the above four categories. Therefore, when you take care of the first four types of men, you will minister to this fifth type as well.

APPENDIX D:

Man in the Mirror Bible Study
Table Leader's Job Description

Pat has been teaching the Man in the Mirror Bible study in Winter Park, Florida, for more than twenty years. Below is the job description he uses for his table leaders. Pat studies and puts together a lesson each week. We provide a location, coffee and donuts, and the men. All the leaders have to do is come prepared to facilitate a discussion after Pat speaks.

If you have a weekly men's Bible study, this might be helpful to you as you recruit table or group leaders. Feel free to adapt it to your particular situation.

THE MAN IN THE MIRROR BIBLE STUDY
TABLE LEADER'S JOB DESCRIPTION

- **MAN IN THE MIRROR VISION:** To engage every man in America with a credible offer of Jesus Christ and the resources to grow.
- **MAN IN THE MIRROR MISSION:** To equip leaders who are reaching men.
- **MAN IN THE MIRROR BIBLE STUDY MISSION:** To engage men in Orlando with a credible offer of Jesus Christ, help them grow in knowledge and love for Christ, and equip them to serve God in the home, church, workplace, community, and world.
- **FOCUSING IDEAS:** Shepherd model (versus teaching). We are a disciple-making ministry. We help men change their lives by connecting the dots between the Bible and their daily lives. We measure our profits in changed lives. "Teach these great truths to trustworthy men who will, in turn, pass them on to others" (2 Timothy 2:2 TLB). Make MIM BS a "safe place" for men to come and investigate the claims of Christianity. Do not put pressure on men to conform to certain behavior. Instead, show men Christ.
- **LEADERSHIP:** Leadership consists of two equally important parts: First, participation in leader's discipleship group. Second, your table becomes an outlet for personal ministry.
- **QUALIFICATIONS:** Love for Christ. Faithful (2 Timothy 2:2). Shepherd's heart. True believers in the vision and mission. Want a purpose

greater than self. Plugged into church. Tither (or actively working to get there). Soul winner. Sign statement of faith. Recruit assistant table leader to lead table in your absence; mentor to become a leader in future.

- **MESSAGE:** The greatest contribution we can make to a man is to help him change the core affections of his heart. We are not trying to fix men's behavior. Christianity is not behavior modification; it is heart transformation. Obedience is the overflow of being in the real presence of Jesus.

YOUR OVERARCHING TABLE GOAL FOR THE YEAR:

_____

_____

MAJOR RESPONSIBILITIES:

____**1. PERSONAL HOLINESS:** I agree to endeavor with the Spirit's help to live in a way that recommends my message. If at any time I find myself not walking rightly with my God, I agree to discuss this with Pat Morley. You must be actively involved in a church to be a leader. (Encourage your men to be actively involved in a Bible believing church.)

____**2. LEADER MEETINGS:** I recognize that relationships with fellow table leaders are integral to the continuity and success of our Bible study. I agree to attend the Man in the Mirror Bible study leader meetings. I also agree to attend the annual leader retreat.

____**3. DISCIPLE MAKING:** My table is my personal ministry (five hours per week all-inclusive). I agree to take a primarily disciple-making approach with my men (versus fellowship, current events, counseling). I will seek to lead every man to a personal faith in Jesus Christ and a maturing relationship with Him. I will give an annual table leader report to leadership team on table's spiritual progress using table evaluation worksheet. "Air time for every man every week." "Long-term, low pressure." Hospital for men with broken wings. Discussion facilitators and shepherds, not "teachers." Talk < 25 percent of time.

____**4. SUCCESS FACTORS:** Meet with my men at other times outside of the Bible study, conduct meaningful discussion, call them weekly, pray for them, create a safe place. I agree to pray for and call (or have someone call) each man weekly (his needs, work, family life, walk with Jesus, personal salvation, spiritual growth). Tell your men you pray for them.

___ 5. **SPIRITUAL DISCIPLINES:** Recognizing that it does not improve my record with Christ, I agree to build the following five spiritual disciplines into my life; and on the strength of my example to challenge, encourage, and motivate my men to do the same motivated by a heart filled with gratitude.
  • Consistent Quiet Time (Matthew 14:23; Joshua 1:8)
  • Organized Bible Study (Proverbs 4:23; Romans 12:2; 2 Timothy 3:16–17)
  • Active Church Involvement (Hebrews 10:24–25)
  • Accountable Relationships (Galatians 6:1–2, James 5:16)
  • Personal Ministry (Ephesians 2:10; 2 Timothy 2:2; 1 Peter 4:10–11)

___ 6. **BUILDING RELATIONSHIPS:** I agree to visit one-on-one with each man at least annually over breakfast, lunch, or coffee.

___ 7. **LEADERSHIP DEVELOPMENT:** I agree to identify potential spiritual leaders from my table (FAT—faithful, available, teachable) and to invest in building them for spiritual service, recommending the most promising as table leaders or assistant table leaders.

___ 8. **PUNCTUALITY:** I agree to arrive no later than 6:45 a.m. on Fridays and adjourn promptly at 8:00 a.m.

___ 9. **VISITORS:** I agree to be sensitive and help make "new men" visiting Man in the Mirror Bible study feel cared about (James 2:1–4). I will park in the grassy areas to make way for them. I will help foster a "bringer" culture.

Leadership is a privilege and a responsibility for which God holds those who accept it accountable. It has a price that I agree to pay. The question on the final exam will be, *"Were you faithful?"*
  • *Name* your men before Christ
  • *Measure* your men by the plumb line of Christ
  • *Love* your men by the example of Christ
  • *Grow* your men in the pattern set by Christ
  • *Involve* your men in the service of Christ

I hereby agree to the terms of this job description for a term of one year. If for any reason I determine my commitment has changed, I agree to notify Pat Morley immediately (James 3:1). If I was a leader last year, in the space before each responsibility I have rated my faithfulness last year and pledge myself anew by God's grace to be faithful in each responsibility (4 = very faithful, 3 = mostly faithful, 2 = somewhat faithful, 1 = not faithful).

Print Name: _____

Sign: _____

Date: _____

SUGGESTED READINGS

Christian Literature

Building a Life Changing Men's Ministry, by Steve Sonderman (Minneapolis: Bethany, 1996).

Brothers! by Geoff Gorsuch and Dan Schaeffer (Colorado Springs: NavPress, 1995).

The Church of Irresistible Influence, by Robert Lewis (Grand Rapids: Zondervan, 2001).

Dog Training, Fly Fishing, and Sharing Christ in the 21st Century, by Ted Haggard (Nashville: Thomas Nelson, 2002).

Effective Men's Ministry, ed. by Phil Downer (Grand Rapids: Zondervan, 2002).

Leadership: Influence That Inspires, by Charles Swindoll (Waco, Tex.: Word, 1985).

Men's Ministry Action Plan, by Man in the Mirror (Orlando: self-published). This is a four-session workbook upon which this book is based. It contains a short introduction to many of these concepts.

Men's Ministry in the 21st Century (Loveland, Colo.: Group, 2004).

The Next Generation Leader, by Andy Stanley (Sisters, Ore.: Multnomah, 2001).

The Purpose Driven Church, by Rick Warren (Grand Rapids: Zondervan, 1995).

Rediscovering Church, by Lynne and Bill Hybels (Grand Rapids: Zondervan, 1995) .

Twelve Ordinary Men, by John MacArthur (Nashville: W Publishing Group, 2002).

Why Men Hate Going to Church, by David Murrow (Nashville: Thomas Nelson, 2005).

Business Literature

Amusing Ourselves to Death, by Neal Postman (New York: Penguin, 1985).

Built to Last, by Jim Collins and Jerry Porras (New York: HarperBusiness, 1994).

Focus, by Al Ries (New York: HarperBusiness, 1996).

Good to Great, by Jim Collins (New York: HarperBusiness, 2001).

Permission Marketing, by Seth Godin (New York: Simon & Schuster, 1999).

The Tipping Point, by Malcolm Gladwell (Boston: Little, Brown & Co., 2000).

Let's be honest: It's a war out there!

There are spiritual forces of wickedness that are constantly pulling on you. As a leader, the attacks against your soul are often more intensified. *The Fourth Seed* devotional will be a source of encouragement to keep going, to "hang tough" and stick it out to the end. It will give you key strategies that will help you not just survive the battle but become a victorious, conquering warrior-leader, for the glory of Christ.

NO MAN LEFT BEHIND
CONFERENCE

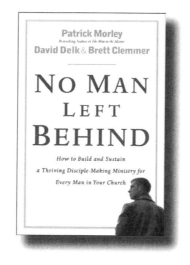

This book is also a training conference available to leaders around the country! Spend two and a half days with pastors and men's ministry leaders working together to apply the *No Man Left Behind* model in each church.

Events are scheduled in Orlando, Los Angeles, Waco, Oklahoma City, and more, with additional cities being added every week! For a complete schedule, or to learn how to bring the *No Man Left Behind* conference to your area, call or visit:

800-929-2536 / www.maninthemirror.org